KU-629-710

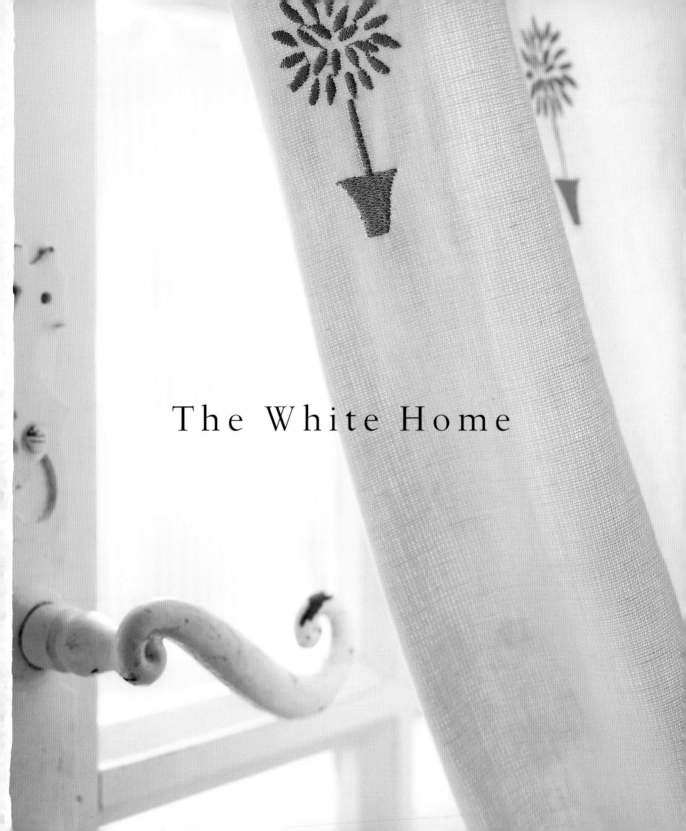

The White Home

The White Home

CREATING ROOMS YOU LOVE TO LIVE IN

Caroline Clifton-Mogg

jacqui small

First published in 2006 by Jacqui Small LLP,
an imprint of Aurum Books Ltd,
25 Bedford Avenue, London WC1B 3AT

PUBLISHER Jacqui Small
EDITORIAL MANAGER Kate John
DESIGNER Ashley Western
EDITOR Sian Parkhouse
PRODUCTION Peter Colley

ISBN 1 903221 59 5

A catalogue record for this book is available
from the British Library.

2008 2007 2006
10 9 8 7 6 5 4 3 2 1

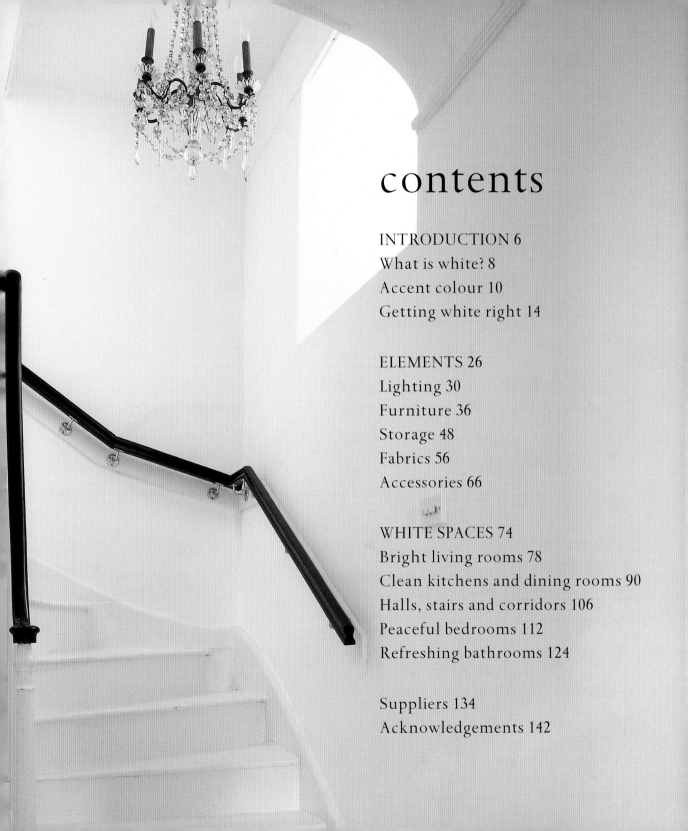

contents

INTRODUCTION 6
What is white? 8
Accent colour 10
Getting white right 14

ELEMENTS 26
Lighting 30
Furniture 36
Storage 48
Fabrics 56
Accessories 66

WHITE SPACES 74
Bright living rooms 78
Clean kitchens and dining rooms 90
Halls, stairs and corridors 106
Peaceful bedrooms 112
Refreshing bathrooms 124

Suppliers 134
Acknowledgements 142

White is the most fascinating, the most subtle, and the most varied colour in the spectrum, and it carries with it many, different associations — on the one hand it is associated with peace and calm, with elegance and sophistication; on the other hand it is linked with freshness and brightness, modernity and innovation. And as contradictory as

these qualities all may seem, they are all correct, for white is all of these things and more.

There is a subtlety in the white decorative palette that makes it a very co-operative colour, ready to move, willingly, in whichever direction you choose; and since the mood of the moment is very much one of clean lightness and space, white suits this feeling perfectly, opening up hidden areas, adding drama to undistinguished spaces, and maximizing all available light .

Through the pages of *The White Home* you will find ways of using white at home in all its myriad ways — on the walls, floors and furniture, at the windows, on the bed. There are white living rooms, bathrooms and kitchens, and in all these spaces, the variations and subtleties to be seen shows that white, far from being the last resort, is, without doubt, the first port of call in any scheme.

Caroline Clifton-Mogg

TOP LEFT An individual interpretation of a white bathroom, dominated by an antique copper bath, furnished with antiques and softened with white lace hangings.

BELOW LEFT Simplicity at a dining table, with distressed painted chairs and table, glazed pottery and old white-glazed tureens.

THIS PAGE A white bedroom with luxuriously dressed bed against a dividing wall. Floor-length unlined curtains are soft and romantic.

WHAT IS WHITE?

White can be cool, white can be warm,

and it is worth identifying in your own mind from the outset of planning any decoration, which tones are which and which palette suits your style.

Cool whites are probably more difficult to handle than warm whites. They are sophisticated shades that need an assured touch. Do not, by the way, confuse cool whites with the once ubiquitous brilliant whites, which have optical brighteners added and lack all sense of subtlety and depth. True cool whites are achieved by combining pure white pigment with a dash of black or blue, and from these are derived such elegant colours as pearl, parchment, alabaster and even putty, all shades much beloved by the French, who use cool whites widely, particularly those touched with grey.

Warm whites, on the other hand are comfortable, luxurious tones. Mark their names: buttermilk, ivory, pale cream — all are associated with the pleasures of life. Soothing and calming, they come from the addition of raw sienna, ochre or other earth pigments, which add their natural warmth to the base tone. Possibly the best and most useful white, which is warm without being hot, is white with just a hint of yellow — a warm hue that is widely, and successfully, used by good decorators in all sorts of decorative schemes.

THIS PAGE Cool whites predominate in this almost minimalist kitchen, where structure, form and, above all, contrast of texture, are all-important.

RIGHT This traditional kitchen relies on whites from the warmer end of the spectrum for its cosy appeal; antique furniture is combined with painted wood and decorative ceramic pieces

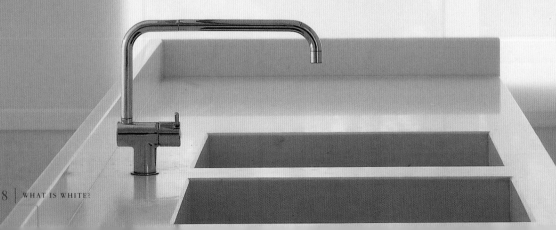

ACCENT COLOUR

Any white room – in fact any room decorated in a
monochrome scheme for that matter – needs accents of colour. Note the
word accents – like accent lighting, accent colours are small punctuations
rather than vast blocks; they are the supporting act, defining the original
colour, highlighting it and giving it additional interest, and it is for you to
decide whether those accents are to be contrasting or toning.

If you have chosen a contrast colour, you will probably want to use even
less than you would with a toning shade. It should be a flash of colour – as
ephemeral as a kingfisher's flight – that will have the most impact – the
lining of a curtain, a pair of cushions, some jewelled-toned ceramics or glass.

If, on the other hand, you want a room made up of tones and shades, the
starting point might be a broken or soft white that has in it yellow or pink
tones. These soft whites bring out the best in warm, relatively soft colours,
and in turn these shades reflect and complement the white base. Again, use
them with parsimony; it is always easy to add, far more difficult to subtract;
start with a mere touch of colour, consider the effect, and then bring in
more, both in quantity and depth until the right balance is achieved.

FAR LEFT Simple curtains are printed with a design of softly faded roses – a subtle contrast against a white background.

LEFT In a Scandinavian room, sharp clear reds highlight soothing whites.

THIS PAGE A room of tone and texture has all the elements within the same colour range, except for the dramatic flash of floral colour in the centre.

CALM AND PEACEFUL, BRIGHT
AND WARM – THE WHITE HOME
IS FLEXIBLE ENOUGH TO BE
WHATEVER YOU WISH IT TO BE,
WHATEVER YOU WANT TO MAKE IT

RIGHT Gentle, diffused light - the sort that is most suitable for a bedroom - is encouraged by hanging sheer white curtains at both the bed and window.

GETTING WHITE RIGHT

ABOVE In this spare contemporary kitchen, the shiny white lacquer surface of the island unit helps to both reflect and bounce the daylight back.

White is, in itself, irrevocably associated with light. Used on its own, it makes spaces appear brighter and larger, and used in conjunction with good lighting – both natural or artificial –it is a powerful, illuminating tool. White is of course reflective and maximizes any available light – which is the good news; the bad news is that it also draws attention to any defects or deficiencies in the room. White magnifies the effect of natural light, making the most of it, reflecting it and bouncing it back. In countries where the natural light is brighter than bright, and where therefore the shadows are deeper than deep, white, often traditionally considered to be the obvious colour for walls and furniture in very sunny climates, actually emphasizes the contrast, in a harsh, unpleasing way; better by far are softer and subtler shades, that temper the strong contrasts. In more temperate climes, if the light in a room is cold – that is, coming from the north or east – then warmer shades of white will be more successful; the opposite applies of course – in south- and west-facing rooms cooler tones can be used. It is important to take these natural aspects into account when decorating with

THIS PAGE So much light pours into this room, and is reflected back, that the large windows have full-length blinds to soften what might otherwise be overwhelmingly bright.

RIGHT A small, wood-floored kitchen has been turned into something special with white paint on every surface, and only the greenery outside for contrast.

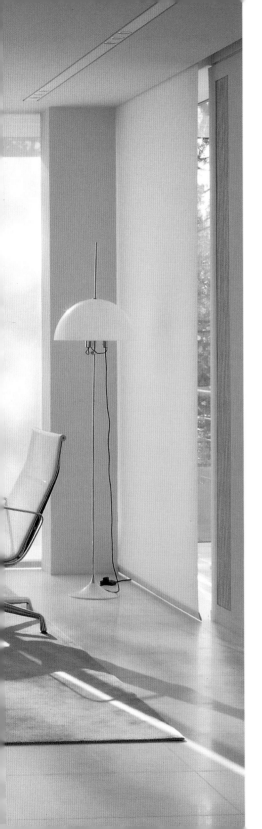

white, more than when using colours (although all wall colours should be chosen with regard to and after visual research into the natural light therein). Natural light is also affected by the outside world: urban light, affected by structural man-made mass from buildings to road surfaces, is flatter, and of quite a different quality from the light in rural areas – who has not remarked on the clearer, often palpably softer, light in the open countryside? – so the wider landscape should always be taken into account. If the light is too strong or harsh, it can be tamed and directed by filtering it through semi-opaque, or slatted blinds.

USING DIFFERENT MATERIALS

Most artists and decorators, following the example of the late, great colourist John Fowler, will use, in a white room, more than one shade of white – he used up to ten shades, some pure, some broken, some off-white. It pays to vary the finish as well as the tone if you are following this route – some powdery and matt, some with a soft sheen and a few – just a few – with gloss.

Use deeper whites to represent or emphasize shading, and remember that all whites take on the tones of other colours and objects around them.

When a room is decorated using white as the base colour, it has the effect of softening and even reducing some of the sharper angles and lines, neutralizing them to a degree. This means that the architectural materials that are used in the white house are of the utmost importance, as they give back definition to the overall scheme, as well as adding interest and contrast. The choice today of materials is wide indeed, from stone and concrete to brick and terracotta; there are any number of metals, including zinc, chrome, steel, aluminium and iron that work well within a white room; glass, plastic,

LEFT Angles and corners, as well as small dramatic features such as the fireplace cut out of a false wall, add striking architectural interest to this primalily white living room.

THIS PAGE Staircase or sculpture? Its architectural elements combine with natural light to add both contrast and ever-changing patterns against the canvass of the white walls.

rubber, and new synthetic materials such as Corian, as well as resin based ones. Last, but certainly not least, there is wonderful wood – so wide in its variety of colour and pattern, so adaptable and accommodating.

TEXTURE AND SURFACES

As with every other element of the white home, it is a question of choosing materials which have the right qualities and appearance, as well as the right texture – always vital in a monochrome scheme. Architectural materials can be used in many different ways in the white home: as walls or room dividers, fireplaces and staircases; all these are vital architectural elements. But perhaps none is more important than the floor – the area where the choice of material has the most impact and most visual importance.

The floor may be of wood, sanded, painted or bleached; it may be stone or ceramic, concrete, rubber; or it may be a combination of surfaces, used in different areas to define different spaces. Some flooring materials, such as

ABOVE LEFT A large space, broken into different areas that perform different functions, is united by the brilliance of the shining white floor.

LEFT In a white corridor, a simple unit is attached 'floating' to the wall. The composition is grounded by the strong lines of the black and white pot.

RIGHT In this more traditional white room, with many different tones and textures within it, the device of the white floor ties every different element together.

limestone or marble, although beautiful, dominate within a white room, almost demanding that the room revolves around them. Too large an area of stone, or for that matter concrete or a smooth surface like rubber, can be cold and should be broken up with rugs or mats. Other materials, particularly wood, are easier: floorboards, new or old can be sanded, polished, painted or limed; they can also be used as a base for other woods or wooden sheet floorings, and wood is one of the best backgrounds for rugs and carpets.

Texture, too, is important. Although the idea of using different textures in a room is to provide contrast, it is important the contrast is pleasing and gives interest: nothing could be duller than a combination of materials that is monotone and without depth. Shiny should be balanced with rough, soft with hard, smooth with rough, whether you are combining hard materials with each other, or introducing soft materials – textiles – to the mix.

LEFT A textured natural floor, in this case brick, is a warm foil for the many different, contrasting whites in the room.

THIS PAGE In a personal and idiosyncratic white room, the polished old brick floor is an integral part of the whole scheme.

THIS PAGE In what was once an industrial unit, what could be more appropriate in a room furnished with semi-industrial furniture, than to have white-painted floorboards?

Painted Floorboards

- Preparation, preparation, preparation! Remove loose paint, before applying new.

- Sand boards lightly before taking further steps.

- Use wood filler for gaps and small holes.

- Base coats and primers help to protect the wood.

- A final coat of lacquer gives extra strength to the finish.

Painted floorboards are not new - they are almost as old as floorboards themselves; they were, however, brought to an art form in early American interior design when resourceful settlers used the wood that surrounded them for everything within the house, sometimes painting the floor with single colours, but also decorating them with more complex patterns. A simple one-colour floor is very effective. There are specialist floor paints available - formulas that are tougher than those for painting walls - but many people prefer the wider range of colours in interior paints. An eggshell or oil-based paint is harder to apply, but it is harder wearing; vinyl emulsion, on the other hand, is quick and easy, but shows wear faster. It all depends which look you prefer.

ABOVE Here white painted boards are a foil to the sophistication of the klismos style chair.

RIGHT A simple room is made sophisticated by using neutral tones, including the painted floor.

Elements

The many different elements of a room – the furniture, the fabrics, the lighting, the storage solutions, and of course the necessary accessories and decorative details – are the all-important parts in any scheme, whether it be one of simplicity or complexity; they are the building blocks which, when put together, make up the complete whole. It is important therefore that each separate element is not only interesting and appealing in itself, as well as serving its particular purpose efficiently, but also that each separate part adds both interest and meaning to the finished room. Using tones of white in a space is a fascinating and complex exercise, but to combine these different, necessary elements in a white-centred scheme is one that requires a subtle approach and an element of compromise. Of course, not every part of a white room should be white – white should be the predominant feeling rather than the predominant colour, and for this reason it is important, not to say essential, to combine other tones and other textures into the overall mix, injecting texture and softness from portable elements such as rugs and carpets, upholstery and drapery.

TOP LEFT Textiles are important; these white curtains are in the simplest of styles, edged with black and hung with black rings on long black poles.

TOP RIGHT How to accessorize white on white: a collection of plaster and alabaster lamp, bust and boxes on a white-topped table.

CENTRE LEFT Mixing white crockery of different styles and in different glazes means that storage can also be display.

CENTRE RIGHT Old wooden furniture painted white looks all the better for a few honourable scars of earlier battles left on view.

BOTTOM LEFT The simplicity of a white loose cover, tied in knots at the side, lends an air of sophistication to the plainest chair.

BOTTOM RIGHT Simplicity and form are the key to good-looking white storage, like these ultra-shallow shelves, neatly divided into shirt-size compartments.

LIGHTING

It is comparatively rare these days that a reception room has only one source of lighting in the form of a single overhead light — but anyone who has sat in a room illuminated in this manner will recognize the way in which, beyond the small, central over-bright cone of light, many areas of the room will be thrown into shadow, and those which are illuminated will be murky and muddy. This is light, not lighting, which is not at all the same thing, for lighting is all-important in a room, and even more all-important in a white room; it is the lighting that gives a room its warmth, friendliness and charm, lighting that sets the mood, renders a colour scheme successful, lighting that essentially makes a room work and heightens our perceptions of the immediate space around us.

This is why a variety of lighting is so important and, like the other elements of the white room, it is a good idea to identify what types of lighting you will need before thinking about the specific lighting fixtures themselves. The field of lighting design is today so complex and so technical, that unless you have some expertise in that field, it is extremely difficult for the amateur

ABOVE A curved wall light, made in traditional parchment and decorated with bold stitching that echoes the lines of the tongue-and-grooved wall.

RIGHT 'Duplex', a brushed stainless steel adjustable table lamp , is a modern classic with a multitude of uses in the contemporary white home, designed by Andrée Putman.

FAR RIGHT A table lamp based on the cone form is as simple as a sculpture, but as useful as a lamp.

THIS PAGE A frivolity of a table lamp, with its spiralling metal base, and white embroidered shade trimmed with black ribbon.

to give precise specifications for any lighting scheme. There are systems that add varying coloured washes to a wall, or alter the tones of the lighting according to the time of day; there is fibre-optic lighting, LED lighting, remote-controlled lighting, lighting that gives a light equivalent to day-light and lighting that gives a whiter light – in fact, almost any effect and any combination you might want is possible. It is a science and an art, and it rightly treated as such by many lighting designers, whose schemes will provide the right amount of effective contrast within all the elements of a room while making it a pleasant environment in which to live. Generally speaking, this side of the lighting conundrum is not for the amateur – but what one can usefully do, however, is identify what sort of finished effect you are looking for, and what areas of lighting are important to you.

Generally speaking, there are three main types of lighting. Task lighting, as its name implies, is tightly defined lighting that illuminates particular activities – cooking, sewing, reading and so on – and which could range from directional spotlights set in cooker hoods, ceilings and walls to portable spots attached to furniture or an anglepoise lamps set on a desk.

CONTROLLING THE LIGHT, WHETHER IT COMES STREAMING IN THROUGH THE WINDOW, OR IS SOURCED FROM A SERIES OF LAMPS, IS PROBABLY THE MOST IMPORTANT FACTOR IN A WHITE INTERIOR

Ambient lighting is background lighting, which is not at all the same thing as dull, boring lighting. Ambient lighting literally creates the ambience of a room, with lights that define the space, and might range from up and down-lighters to decorative table and floor lamps. Ambient lighting can be used to diffuse and accentuate, and it should be very carefully used in a white-toned room as white will reflect and return the light.

There is also accent or display lighting, lighting that, as the name implies, is used to focus on a particular thing – an object, a picture, or perhaps a piece of furniture; accent lighting can also be used as a tool to bring forward one particular element of a room, such as a fireplace, while concealing another.

SITING AND SELECTING LIGHT FITTINGS

The initial stage of thought for any lighting scheme is to think about what activities you want to pursue in which room and what areas you want singled out; also to think about where tables and chairs are to be positioned, and where in an ideal world you would like specific lights – an architect's tip is, when considering a lighting scheme, to use Post-it notes wherever you think you might like a lamp or an electrical point, which you can then add to or

ABOVE An oversized ceiling light, like a giant mother-ship, that will softly diffuse the light in an all-white room.

BELOW A Japanese paper lantern wall light, hung here against a rough brick wall; the variation in textures is intriguing.

BELOW RIGHT 'Jack', a floor light designed by Tom Dixon, is a graphic piece of three-dimensional art, enjoyed at its best when placed on a floor of a contrasting colour.

re-position as new ideas come to mind. All this groundwork is for the lighting scheme in general rather than lighting in particular, and your other most useful contribution will be the choice of specific lamps and fixtures. This is an area which has developed enormously in the last twenty years — many modern lights are designed almost as sculptural objects and they can play as important a part in the look of a room as a painting or a piece of furniture, so it is important to look at as many different styles and designs as possible.

Lighting is one area where the old and the new can be very successfully combined: antique table lamps — perhaps converted from old vases or candelabra — work very well with sharp-edged lighting fixtures; it is the final effect which counts, and that must always be to make the lit space both welcoming and effective. And one last thought — possibly the most useful addition to any lighting scheme is a set of dimmers; that way you can, at small cost, become your own lighting designer with ease.

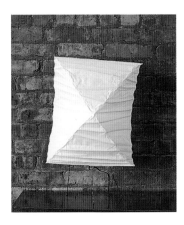

F U R N I T U R E

Furniture is probably the most important

element of any room – due to its relative size of course, but also due to its
suitability for any given space. It is all too easy to take furniture for granted –
it's there, it does its job, it can be more or less ignored. But a successful room,
and the successful arrangement of a room, relies on each piece of furniture
being viewed first in isolation, really looked at as to its shape, design and size,
and then thought about in relation to everything else within that room, from
the other pieces of furniture to rugs, curtains, pictures and decorative
objects. In other words, furniture should not be taken for granted. This is, it
goes without saying, particularly important within a white room where a
harmony of shades, shapes and textural qualities are vital to the overall effect.

Scale is all important, and that should be cubic scale rather than just the
amount of floor space a piece takes up. Next to scale comes balance. A room
feels uneasy when some of the furniture seems top-heavy or too dense, for

 A fluid arrangement
of oversized seating works
well in a white room.

ABOVE Classic and wicker
chairs acquire a modern
look when upholstered or
painted in bright white.

RIGHT This white textured
sofa is part of a geometric
composition that includes
both the picture behind
and the dramatic table.

the eye seeks balance and proportion within a space. It is easy to think that
the only way to balance one chair is with another of equal weight or bulk, but
balance comes in many forms — a tall bureau might be balanced by a tall
screen or a table with a mirror above it. Balance does not mean equal size or
equal weight; it means density being balanced with equal density. In a room
which is predominantly white, the planned decorative scheme, and the
choice of furniture, may very well not all be upholstered, nor all of wood.
Many white rooms will contain pieces that combine metal, glass, wood,
laminates or even stone, and although all these different materials can work
very well together, they carry different densities which means that the
overall balance of the room will also be different. A table, for instance, that

THIS PAGE In this all-purpose living room a carefully positioned, oversized white sofa delineates the different functions of the space.

you can see through – metal, glass or Perspex, perhaps, will not carry the same weight as a similarly sized piece in solid wood; if they are placed relatively close together, the former will need something extra to give it the same importance – a mirror or painting hung above it, or solid objects, decorative or otherwise, displayed on the surface. A room that is satisfying to the eye will have taken these aspects into consideration.

WOODEN FURNITURE

Painted wood is particularly effective in the white room, and it can be an economical way of achieving light and graceful form. Furniture made from cheap woods such as beech or pine take very well to being painted – indeed the ubiquitous stripping of old pine furniture, so prevalent some ten years ago, was in fact incorrect, because such pieces, when first made, were nearly

TOP LEFT Different tones of white-toned wood are brought together in the panelling and painted door.

LEFT A traditional Swedish room, with the white enamel stove and all the wooden furniture painted in different tones of white.

ABOVE Worn areas of paint are left unrestored to let the grain of the wood show on this antique dresser.

THIS PAGE A simply furnished room has been made charming by painting everything in sight white – from the mirror to the table and chair and even the floor.

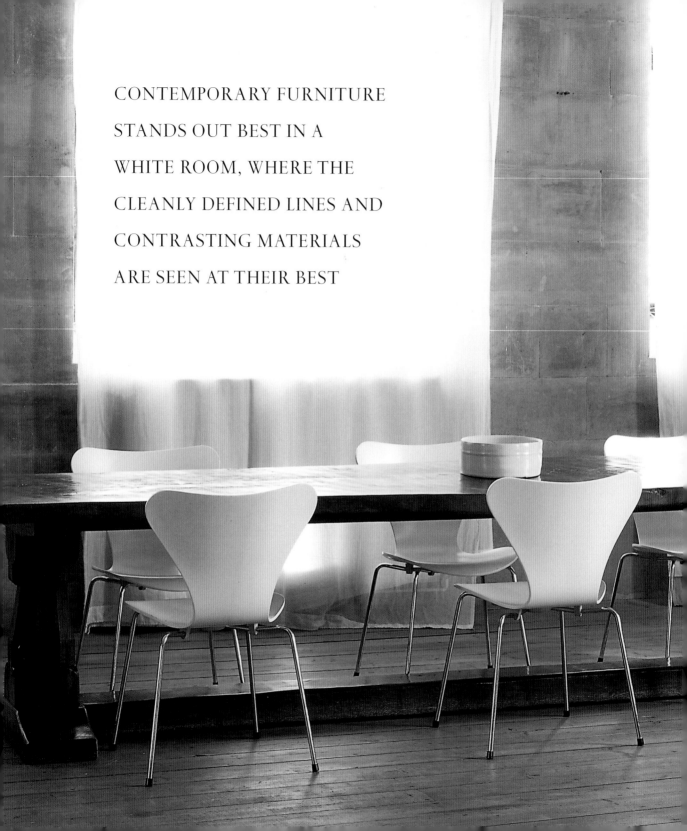

CONTEMPORARY FURNITURE
STANDS OUT BEST IN A
WHITE ROOM, WHERE THE
CLEANLY DEFINED LINES AND
CONTRASTING MATERIALS
ARE SEEN AT THEIR BEST

always painted. If you are thinking of painting an old piece, rather than something newly made, it is interesting to reflect the age and history of the piece, no matter how humble its origin; one option might be to coat it lightly so that the original wooden finish shows through in places; another option is to apply several layers of paint, perhaps using slightly different tones, which are then rubbed back to give an impression of softly graded colour.

Contemporary furniture can be a combination of almost any material, from granite and concrete to marble and slate; leather and suede to stainless steel and aluminium; there are no elements that could not be included in the modern white room, and the important thing is to make sure no one material dominates – hard with soft, rough with smooth is the rule. Thus, metal and glass or marble and slate should be tempered with suede, rough-textured linens or woven velvet. Temper furniture with objects and pictures that are pleasing in their own right, and the total effect will be one of air and space.

LEFT In an early 19th-century church converted into a dwelling, these white moulded chairs from the 1950s stand out against the dark wood floor.

ABOVE RIGHT White mesh chairs and an Eileen Gray chrome and glass table are as lightweight as the all-white room.

RIGHT The clean lines of the bright white Eero Saarinen chairs and the striking circular table are emphasized by their all-white surroundings.

THIS PAGE This chairs in this white-painted set have distinctive seat covers – each one different but taken from the same family of patterns.

Painted Wooden Chairs

- Always sand wooden chairs thoroughly and fill nicks with filler. Primer is a good base

- Experiment with colours: try a base colour that differs slightly from the top coat, and rub the top coat down when dry to reveal the first.

- Paint the seats a contrasting colour – or several.

- A coat of matt varnish will help to protect the paint.

When the decorator Syrie Maugham painted the furniture in her white room to go with the surroundings (see page 78), commentators expressed shock, but she was in fact reviving a fashion for painted furniture that had been extremely popular in Europe during the 18th and 19th centuries. Around a table, it is still a wonderful way to unify a mis-matched set, or to rescue what might otherwise be considered ordinary in the extreme. If using chairs of different design, ensure every chair is roughly the same height and paint them in a uniform hue. If the room is predominantly white, paint the chairs another colour, to complement or contrast with the subtlety of the surroundings. If you do use white, explore some of the softer tones available.

ABOVE Painting these bar chairs white brings them firmly into the overall scheme of a kitchen.

RIGHT A very ordinary chair, the likes of which can be found in any junk shop, acquires style when painted white.

STORAGE

As well as the practical pieces that we now need around us to function, from cooking utensils to electrical equipment, everyone also has belongings, and most people have more than they think – daily necessities, personal belongings, knick-knacks, and all those things which must be kept even though they are not often used; many, if not most of these need to be kept out of sight. Not many people can operate effectively in an atmosphere of chaos, even if it is controlled chaos, and if you use your home to work in as well as live in then an effective system is essential, and it is extremely satisfying to have a system of storage that works really well for you

It is difficult enough to organize good-looking storage in a multi-hued room, but in a room of white tones, storage must always be of the utmost importance; clutter does not go well in a carefully designed space and it

ABOVE Clever under-stair storage that is almost invisible has been designed to appear as part of the very staircase itself.

RIGHT These built-in cupboards echo other elements in the room, with their flat white expanses and minimal detailing.

THIS PAGE This invisible bedroom storage has flush doors that are painted white without a hint of decorative moulding or excess detail.

LEFT A traditional, white-painted wooden armoire acts as all-purpose storage in this light-filled kitchen that leads into the garden.

RIGHT A clever idea, in a small urban space, is to paint basic shelf units the same white as the walls and then utilize them as open display.

particularly does not go in a carefully designed space that is predominantly white, whether that is white contemporary or white traditional; if there is one thing that is common to all well-designed white-based homes, whether traditional or contemporary, it is that there is never too much clutter on view, for clutter is the antithesis of white and cool and calm.

The first task is to edit your belongings to get rid of the unnecessaries; the second task is to grade the belongings that remain into 'essentialness', based on how close to hand each item has to be, and what you need in each room. Then you can begin to work out what sort of storage is suitable for each group, for the most important thing – if obvious – is that you must know where everything is to be able to find it when you want it. The large cupboard into which everything is just chucked will, in the long run, become just as much of a problem as leaving everything out on the floor.

Storage should fit the style of the room or space that it is in – do not look to buy it independently of everything else; it should be in proportion and in harmony with the rest of the furniture in the room. Built-in storage is one

LEFT A large dresser made to fit the kitchen is the perfect place to store and display all the everyday china, old and new.

THIS PAGE Storage as a statement: this unit has been painted in dramatic black, the better to display shelves of all-white china.

ABOVE A simple system of geometric all-white shelving is perfect for books and objects in an all-white room.

RIGHT These shelves have been made especially to display the large collection of Buddy L-pressed steel model cars made in the 1920's and 30's.

answer but built-in storage in white can sometimes appear overpowering – so rather than just painting it flat white use several different shades, to highlight moulding and panelling to give it depth and contrast. Free-standing storage has the advantage that it can be moved around and also does not look quite so permanent. Treat such piece as furniture – they have to work with the other elements in the room.

DISPLAY STORAGE

This is another option – a room decorated principally in tones of white is the perfect background for books and objects shown on shelves and flat surfaces – perhaps some of the pieces that you are thinking of consigning to the depths of a cupboard would have a new lease of life, displayed on well-made shelves .

Remember that successful storage does not have to consist only of conventional cupboards and shelves; it could be an old shop fitting – glass-fronted drawers from a haberdasher or apothecary for instance. It could be an antique piece – a decorative marriage chest or antique linen press, or even an old school trunk or solicitor's deed box. The more mixture there is, the more the overall look will work. You can incorporate modern baskets, boxes and trunks and chests as well – pieces that have a decorative value as well as a functional one, and that can double as tables or stools around the house – they can be mixed in with older and larger pieces, and used in different places when needed.

Storage does not, of course, have to be added to simply every room. In some homes it might make more sense to designate a small room or part of a larger one as an integral storage system – fit drawers and shelves that will take everything from books to clothes as well as objects that you don't use every day, leaving only the room-by-room necessities to be stored in situ.

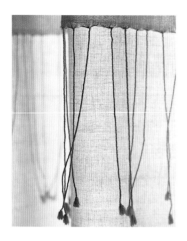

FABRICS

The range of fabrics available today – design, composition, colour – is absolutely vast and the difference between fabrics designed for the fashion and the interior markets becomes more blurred with every passing year. In the white home, fabrics are essential, both to add a necessary softness to the overall, potentially frosty, scheme, and to provide texture – texture is a very necessary element of a white decorative scheme.

Combining different weights of textile works very well. A curtain in one white-based design can have narrow borders of another, complementary design added in horizontal bands across the bottom of the curtain. Or, at the window, a full-length white cotton sheer voile curtain beneath a white or natural linen looks immediately luxurious and soft; added colour is not needed. And while on the subject of sheer or lightweight fabrics such as voile or muslin, it is important when using them to allow a generous, even over-generous amount of fabric in making up curtains: lightweight fabrics need to billow rather than flap disconsolately – better to use a greater quantity of a cheaper fabric than to be parsimonious with an expensive one.

ABOVE RIGHT A wood-panelled window is framed by a curtain in natural linen held in place with a cotton and linen tassel.

RIGHT Narrow panels of fabric are used as curtains and attached by small rings to a narrow pole.

FAR RIGHT An elaborate curtain contrived to seem simple, is caught by heavy loops onto a black pole.

BELOW The ultimate white bedroom; crisp white cotton pillowcases and sheets against a white background, hung with decorative pictures.

Alluring and welcoming, cool and fresh, and usually crisp – this last is a word often used to describe natural fabrics such as linen, ticking and cotton, and if you use these fabrics unadorned and undecorated, they should indeed be crisp; one of the essentials of the white home is that every element remains white, and that means clean and pressed, for nothing looks worse than dirty, or even vaguely grubby, fabric. This is why many of the textiles in the white house are loose covers and curtains that can be easily removed and cleaned.

White and cream textiles – and other natural shades that move away from white but which remain within the same palette – can also be heavy, rich and luxurious; think of the deep pile of cotton or silk velvet, the depth of

ABOVE In an otherwise restrained bedroom, antique lace-trimmed pillows add a subtly feminine touch.

RIGHT This bed is hung with checked sheer muslin, dressed with a selection of decorative pillows made from vintage textiles with just a hint of colour.

ABOVE The upholstered wing chair and the neat seat covers of the upright chairs are in striking contrast to the uneven floor and woodwork .

PREVIOUS PAGES This iron day bed is certainly striking, dressed with antique pillows massed on a sheepskin-covered seat.

the new suede fabrics, heavy silks, felt and wool. Curtains or upholstery in these fabrics bring a completely different look to the white home – one of unashamed sybaritic living, of tactile warmth and of relaxed sophistication. Woven and self-patterned designs are another important weapon in the textile arsenal; by combining several of these in a room with other simpler fabrics, you build up a depth of texture and visual interest.

CUSHIONS AND THROWS

The popularity of throws, cushions and rugs in a contemporary space is due to their ability to add instant contrast and interest to an otherwise monotone interior. Go either for the shock of the strong and the bold, or try a gentler contrast using natural shades, from creams to putty and taupe. There are different textural moods to be considered – simple woven materials like natural linens, calicos, muslins and narrow striped tickings point towards a simple, slightly rustic, look, while self-patterned damasks, intricate weaves

ABOVE Small fragments of colourful antique and vintage fabrics are made into the central panels of otherwise white cushions.

ABOVE RIGHT This sofa has been draped with part of a collection of old linen , including tablecloths, sheets and decorative cut-work pieces.

and smooth woven silks are more formal. The scale of the design is also important : if you are combining patterns and weaves, combine also the scale of the designs, mixing large with small, busy with restrained.

There is a place also in the white home for antique and vintage fabrics, particularly for old linen sheets and tablecloths. Many of these were highly ornamental, decorated either with cutwork or embroidered monograms and other designs, and they can be used in both a contemporary and traditional fashion. A double linen sheet, for example can be used as a sofa throw; a fragment that includes a monogram can be used as a striking chair back; and floor-length slipcovers can cover dining chairs. At the window also, the dark corners of the linen cupboard come into their own: old linen sheets, whether they are coarse or fine, can be used as curtains; they can be sewn to slip over metal rods or simply hung with the border acting as an informal pelmet. Old linen towels, particularly those with fringed edges, can be made into blinds or simple curtains for small windows. The choice is endless.

ABOVE LEFT AND RIGHT
Straight-backed wicker
chairs have been dressed
with plain white linen loose
covers, edged and tied with
a neat navy blue border
and navy ribbons.

LEFT Long, white tailored
loose covers give an
instantly formal air to
this light dining room.

RIGHT White fancy and
feminine seat covers make
these curved back chairs
look like ballerinas.

Loose Covers

- If you have never made covers, practise with muslin.

- If the chairback is not upholstered, attach batting to give more bulk.

- Choose a material that can be cleaned or washed – and pre-wash before making up

- Loose covers are by their nature informal, so avoid elaborate or heavy fabrics.

Loose covers were originally designed as dust-covers – to be used on chairs that had been upholstered with valuable or fragile fabrics. Often put on in large houses when the family was not in residence, they found favour as an adaptable way of furnishing a room, with winter and summer covers often being made for the same piece. In Scandinavia, wooden dining chairs were often finished with loose cotton covers. The most effective loose covers are those which look as crisp as a newly starched handkerchief and which are attached to the chair accordingly. There are various styles, ranging from the all-enveloping top-to-toe look to a piece that merely covers the seat, and it is a good idea to drape some fabric over a chair before deciding which style looks best.

ABOVE The plain linen cover over the back and seat emphasizes the elegant reeded legs of this balloon-back Regency-style chair.

ACCESSORIES

There is always a place for the decorative, even in the simplest, most pared-down, whitest of spaces – and indeed if decorative details are not added those simple spaces, no matter how carefully and imaginatively planned, will merely be dull, without redeeming life or colour. Accessories and decorative details are the fastest way to add the personality to a room – how often does one remark disparagingly that somewhere 'looks like a hotel room', meaning that there are no personal touches or anything quirky or interesting to be seen, that the room is dreary and without flavour.

White is the colour of display, par excellence – set against a white background, every accessory, every object stands out in sharp relief, which is of course a good thing, but it does mean that what you display and how and where you display it should be thought about with great care.

ABOVE RIGHT The fragility of white-glazed cups and saucers contrasts with the rougher texture of the earthenware tiles.

RIGHT Against a sepia-toned wallpaper, a collection of early English creamware stands out.

FAR RIGHT An ornamental ewer which stands alone on a dark table top is both striking and decorative.

OPPPOSITE These dishes and plates have been collected from diverse sources and hung to make an interesting composition.

THIS PAGE This Rosenthal teaset was owned by the Bauhaus designer Walter Gropius, who admired its functional beautiful lines.

FAR RIGHT The light white glaze of this bowl and plate, with the clay deliberately showing through, gives a delicate beauty to the design.

THE UNIVERSAL SIMPLICITY
AND PURITY OF WHITE
CHINA, WHATEVER ITS
PERIOD OR DESIGN, MAKES
IT EASY TO MIX DIFFERENT
PIECES TOGETHER

ABOVE A simple pitcher,
once strictly functional,
when filled with dried
white hydrangea flowers
becomes decorative.

Any object or group of objects can be the subject of a display, from the purely decorative – ceramic and glass ware, paintings or sculpture – to the originally utilitarian, from new jugs to antique saucepans. It is entirely to do with what you choose to gather and how you group them together.

A group is anything more than one, and a collection could comprise as few as two objects, which means that many people, unknowingly, own the nucleus of a collection without knowing it; look around your home to see what you have dotted around on shelves or in cupboards – it is very likely that you already have the basis of an effective and interesting display.

INJECTING COLOUR

You might think that a white background denotes caution in the choice of colour or shape you can display, but there is no reason to stick to the unexceptional or the safe and therefore dull; you can explore the use of bold coloured accessories, for example. The contrast between strong colour and white is always attention seeking – just make sure to use them in moderation; start with just one piece – a bright red bowl, a gleaming black vase – and see how it works in the room; build on the basis of your success, add another and then another, and step back and look after each addition – learn when to stop and when to go on. White against white itself, although

not as easy to get right, can also be highly effective, particularly if you choose sharp textural contrasts such as shiny white lacquer or heavy white marble.

HOW TO GROUP OBJECTS

Effective display comes from intelligent grouping and the basic rules – which can be amended as much as you like – are either to group pieces by shape, colour, material. Pieces of clear glass, or dense terracotta, for example, look wonderful massed together, even if each piece is very different in design from its neighbour; a collection of teapots or wooden boxes gain when arranged together, and a grouping of all things red – or yellow, or green – becomes much stronger when shown in one setting. Lighting is all important in display – particularly when the background is as uncompromising as white; you may care to light a display with ambient background light, or you may prefer very tight accent lighting that highlights the most meaningful items; it is a question of preference for immediate or long-term impact.

And finally remember flower power, the easiest and quickest way to add instant decorative detail to an otherwise all-white interior: depending on the final effect, use flowers that contrast with white, or that subtly reinforce the

OPPOSITE An frivolous collection of objects looks charming brought together and hung against a white-painted wall.

ABOVE LEFT Varied tones of white are illustrated here, with the contrasting textures of a plaster figure next to an elaborately carved stone urn.

ABOVE RIGHT In this bathroom, the combination of old iron table, painted mirror and old towel rail, all painted white, makes an interesting composition.

BELOW an oversized white bowl is a sculptural object framed by a dark fireplace.

RIGHT A composition of miniature porcelain figures, candlesticks, a pot stand and platters show the variations that can be found in white ceramics.

background shade. Do not dismiss the use of white flowers on their own; it was the famous florist Constance Spry who, in the 1950s, brought to the attention of a 20th-century audience the beauty of white flowers used as a single colour block, one species in combination with each other, with no other distraction save the element of green in stalks and the occasional leaf. The effect is just as powerful today.

White Spaces

A white room is a room without conditions: shading it and furnishing it in tones of white allows a freedom that a room decorated in brighter, stronger or deeper colours, cannot achieve; indeed white has the enviable power to become anything you want, in a way that a colour – any colour, no matter how subtle – never can.

A white room is a room of calm, whether the decoration be conceived in classical or contemporary style, and when whites are used to define a space, the space can become any and everything that is required at the time – a room with a single, distinct purpose, or one that is multifunctional and multi faceted. White removes physical boundaries and, if the spaces you are decorating are small, white walls will vanish and white floors disappear; and in a larger space, a white palette used with all its variations throughout the house will by definition make the total area seem even more spacious than it really is.

While white can unify a myriad surfaces, it can also act as a background: against a white backdrop, possessions and pieces of furniture stand out, and accents of pure colour make their mark. In every room in the house it has the power to make the best of what is there, and what could be more satisfying than that?

TOP LEFT A bathroom painted white with white tiles makes the most of all available natural light.

TOP RIGHT Minute, but as cosy as a cabin: all-white walls and luxurious white linen are very welcoming.

CENTRE LEFT An all-in-one kitchen on a single wall is concealed behind doors with push-touch mechanisms.

CENTRE RIGHT An all-white sitting room is dramatized by the addition of a central dark, shaggy rug.

BOTTOM LEFT A long white room with few soft furnishings is softened by full sheer curtains at the window.

BOTTOM RIGHT Uncompromisingly, this long white trough-like sink is striking in its simplicity.

BRIGHT LIVING ROOMS

Even seventy-five years later, it is really not possible to write about the idea of a white living room without mentioning the much-noted drawing room designed in 1932 by Syrie Maugham for her own house in Chelsea, London: much talked of at the time, it was a perfect symphony of white, combining themes of such subtle tones as ivory, parchment, pearl and oyster. Traditional decorators in the early 20th century rarely designed rooms based on tone-on-tone neutral schemes, preferring those that depended on

RIGHT This sitting room tempers its whiteness with natural linens and soft pink-based hues, notably in the blinds and kelim rug.

RIGHT Comfortable and classical, all the furniture in tbis living room is in tones of white and highlighted with carefully chosen accessories.

THIS PAGE In a room of visual and aesthetic interest the white is tempered and accentuated with flashes of contrast colour and shape.

BELOW RIGHT A restored marble fireplace makes a dramatic centrepiece in an otherwise uncompromising contemporary setting.

contrast and striking use of pattern, and Mrs Maugham's scheme caused much comment at the time; today, however, when looking at photographs of the room, what strikes the eye is just how very conventional it now seems. It is very pretty of course, with its matching white sofas, heavily textured white rug and low white screen (behind which the dissonant black piano was hidden), but hardly shocking – and it is that fact that shows just how much influence, both in terms of decoration and design, that that room had on English interior decoration of the time, as well as in the decades since.

MODERNISM

In Europe, during the same period, white as a liberating colour in the interior decorating palette was also being used, but in a completely different way from the well-mannered English style. Bright, clean white was seen as an almost integral element of the work produced by the architect and designers working first at the Bauhaus School in Dessau, Germany in the 1920s and early 1930s and later, in America and Britain. Designers like Walter Gropius, the founder and director of the Bauhaus movement, relished the clarity and freshness of pure white as a background for the clean, ascetic lines of their

furniture and textile designs; and the materials they were experimenting with – glass, stainless steel, formica, and laminated plywood – were triumphantly highlighted against a cool white. Both these approaches influence and inform our approach to white today, and although the contemporary white living room is without doubt a little softer, a little easier than an austere Bauhaus room, and a little edgier, a little more pared down, than a 1930s drawing room, it still is a clean, fresh room, one that breathes air and light, but is in part a sanctuary from the outside world.

LIVING WITH WHITE

Some decorators suggest that, when moving into a new home, important rooms, like sitting rooms, should initially be painted white as a matter of course. The white is used as a 'living with' colour – something that gives you time to see how the room looks in different lights, and what sort of shades you will feel most comfortable living with. This approach does white, in all its

ABOVE The all-white surroundings of this Manhattan room are emphasized by the display of early American weathervanes.

RIGHT The seemingly haphazard way in which the books are stored gives an informal aspect to this predominantly white room.

various guises, a disservice, for it is very much more than a holding pattern; indeed, one of the simplest of ways to update a living room is to take out every piece of furniture and every object, paint the room in your chosen shades of white, and then just see how much of the furniture and bit , which seemed before to be absolutely essential, you actually need to put back in your new, white room; white and clutter, white and confusion do not go well together.

Light, whether natural or artificial, affects very much the way that white appears on the walls, and it is always worthwhile buying and trying sample sizes of different tones in situ before you make your final choices. The word is used in the plural because the white sitting room, to be successful, is not, of course, painted in only one shade; in a room of such varied purpose at least three shades will be needed, perhaps more – try them all, with each other and in different lights, thinking about woodwork as well as the walls.

BRINGING IN COLOUR

But however many shades of white you choose for the initial scheme, most white rooms, particularly multi-purpose ones like the modern living room, are improved with a dash of colour, whether that be in the initial colour scheme or through the objects and furnishings. Most white rooms will in fact appear whiter if other colours are added – either soft tones that have white as a base colour, or small, sharp doses of stronger colours that throw the whiteness into relief. All colours are affected by their surroundings, and white more than most – try a piece of white-painted card next to the colour you are thinking of using with it – a colour of strong contrast will make white appear brighter, and a soft shade will make the white become softer, almost less white. Try out dashes of the sort of colours or tones that you are thinking of, as many of them will look very different in such circumstances. On the 'less is more' principle, and depending on the

LEFT Echoing the lines of the Arts and Crafts style, the elements of this black and white room are disciplined and severe.

RIGHT In an almost all-white room, colour and softness are added with the inclusion of a mini-woodland glade.

size and shape of the room, one contrast colour is probably enough and too little is better than too much – addition is always easier than subtraction.

In a sitting room, a white palette – indeed, any neutral palette – will only work well where there is enough contrast of light and shade, a contrast which can be achieved both through lighting and through the use of different, contrasting textures in any textiles and furnishings. These are of the utmost importance in an all-white sitting room, where care must be taken to see that the overall impression is not one of an inhospitable chill. Soft furnishings add softness and depth, but they do not necessarily have to be white or even off-white –

for many people that is simply not a practical option, and, although whites does look wonderful, it is very high maintenance. Think instead of a more neutral tone or a self-patterned fabric, using throws in different textures and different weights – some white, some coloured; other ways to add colour might be through rugs, bright bowls of flowers, and floor and table lamps.

Lighting is, of course, as important in the all-white sitting room as it is in every other space, and a mixture of lighting is required, both as background and for specific activities; vary the height of individual lamps and try out shades before you buy them as they alter both the quality and tone of the light dramatically.

LEFT Antique furniture from different periods and of different styles are united by the backdrop of sheer full white curtains.

THIS PAGE This extra-deep seat has mirrored feet that are reflected in the floor of poured resin, which has sparkling mother-of pearl added for luminacy.

Embellishing Curtains

- Make sure the two fabrics complement or contrast with each other, rather than fight.

- Use compatible weights – don't use a muslin border on a velvet curtain!

- Remember that if the border is patterned the eye will be drawn directly towards it.

- Pin paper cut to the width of the border to the curtain, then stand back to judge it.

A relatively easy way to embellish existing white curtains – as well as a practical way to add to a pair of curtains that are too short or narrow for a particular window – is to add a border of contrasting colour, either horizontally or vertically. A horizontal border can either be added onto the bottom, if extra length is required, or some distance up the curtain. A vertical border can be applied in the same way – either as an additional drop, or as a contrast band. The most important thing to remember in each case is that the width of the new border must be in proportion to both the length and the width of the existing curtain, and that if the border is edge-to edge on a pair of curtains, that it will not be out of proportion when the curtains are drawn.

RIGHT A simple white Roman blind is lifted with the addition of a broad all-round border in a contrasting tobacco brown.

THIS PAGE A conservatory addition makes this white kitchen one of glass and gloss, emphasized by the white moulded chairs and the glass table.

CLEAN KITCHENS
AND DINING ROOMS

BELOW This kitchen space, which leads into the living area, is lacquered like a culinary jewel box.

BELOW RIGHT A white kitchen is stimulated by the addition of a wooden table and chairs, a multi-coloured rag rug and busy open storage.

When the fitted kitchen first arrived in our lives, there was only one colour to have, and of course it was white: everything from paintwork to units, fridge to cooker, came in shiny, sparkling, bright, white; all-white represented modernity and the modern kitchen was what we all wanted. White had associations with total cleanliness and hygiene – surfaces were wipeable, floors were moppable and the efficiency of the operating theatre and the laboratory was implied, if not actually stated. This seemed the bright future – a far cry from the inefficient, dirt-collecting, old-fashioned kitchens of the past. But, of course, after the

first shock of the new had passed, taste inevitably became broader and today there is room both for kitchens that look like spaceship command posts and those that look like farmhouse living rooms – and every style in between. Whichever style you choose, a kitchen is an expensive room to both build and equip, and once you have expended time and money it is better to have a kitchen that weathers the changing weather of fashion – particularly as far as colour is concerned – which is of course where the white kitchen comes in.

White works both in a traditional kitchen and in one of contemporary design. For first time kitchen makers who have inherited an old but workable kitchen, for those who are working on a budget or indeed for people who like the idea of an unfitted kitchen, made up of pieces that were designed for another purpose, white used on every surface, in different tones ranging from cream to grey, is an instant and immediate way of uniting disparate elements

LEFT A shining, moveable island system has cut-out recesses, echoed in the alcoves in the wall unit.

THIS PAGE A classic white kitchen using traditional elements in a soft and rather modern way.

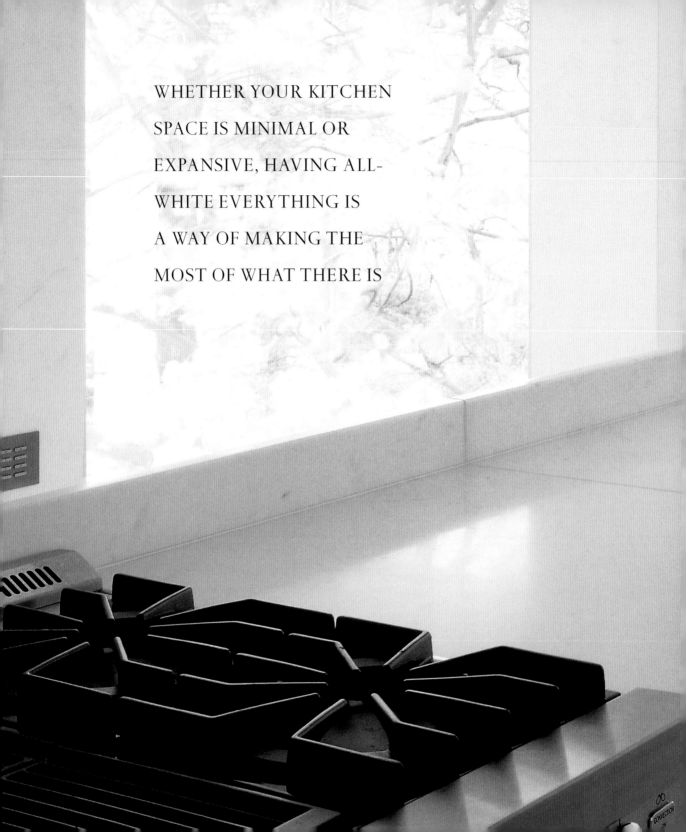

WHETHER YOUR KITCHEN
SPACE IS MINIMAL OR
EXPANSIVE, HAVING ALL-
WHITE EVERYTHING IS
A WAY OF MAKING THE
MOST OF WHAT THERE IS

THIS PAGE Apart from the iron hobs, this kitchen is uncompromisingly white, embellished with a pair of square sinks cut into the marble surface.

as well as creating something unique. Small kitchens, particularly small city kitchens, look slick, sleek and very professional when designed in white, and the quickest way to freshen up a tired or just dull kitchen is to give it a mega-blast of white. Colour also works in a white kitchen, in small sharp bursts which serve to intensify the underlying tones but remember that in most kitchens there is an abundance of natural colours, from fruit and vegetables to crockery and containers.

SELECTING MATERIALS

Surfaces that work with a white kitchen include zinc, white marble, limestone and limed wood. Indeed, the materials that can be used in a white kitchen are myriad. On the floor stone, slate or marble, although expensive, will last for ever and can look magnificent. Polished or rough concrete is increasingly popular, as are resin floors which can be coloured (as can

ABOVE LEFT White enlarges, as is shown in this compact kitchen, which is otherwise kept as utterly simple as possible.

TOP Instead of all-white enclosed units, contrast is achieved with an alcove space beneath the sink for alternative storage.

ABOVE A traditional kitchen where the all-white surrounds are relived by open storage and utensils on permanent display.

concrete) in a wide range of shades and tones. Rather than ceramic tiles, terracotta tiles are warm and welcoming and if you like the appearance of wood, there is not only the real thing, (which should always be well-sealed) but also the look-alike synthetic 'planks' which have come a very long way indeed from woodprint acrylic patterns of the 1960s. Rubber floors – a very Italian look – are more practical than they sound, and linoleum is enjoying a renaissance; this last is an interesting floor covering as it is not only warm underfoot but can be cut and arranged in intricate, almost marquetry like, designs. Whichever you choose should be treated so that it is reasonably easy to clean and does not stain too much with the inevitable spillage.

Worktops in a white kitchen, or in any other kitchen, must be easy to keep clean for both hygienic and aesthetic reasons. It is not unusual today to have a combination of surfaces on a worktop: perhaps an area of end-block maple for chopping, or an area of granite, marble or slate for cool work set

ABOVE LEFT A contrast of old and new: white and stainless steel are set off with a polished wooden floor and an antique chair.

ABOVE Wood and white are always a successful combination, viz the central island worktop and wide-planked oak floor.

THIS PAGE AND RIGHT
This is the kitchen of an
enthusiastic and constant
cook; the gleaming
all-white surroundings -
walls, floor, units and
furniture - make a perfect
background for the display
of utensils and tools that
she uses on a daily basis.

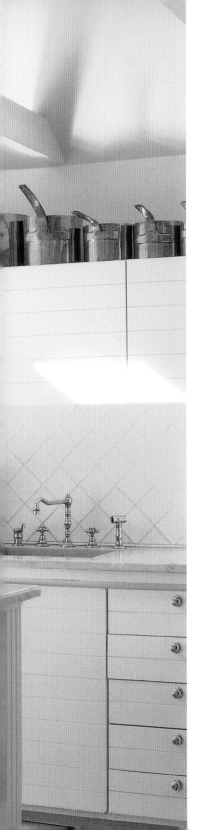

into perhaps a wooden or Corian surface. This last option is an infinitely adaptable material as it can be seamlessly moulded to whatever form is needed, including that of a sink or sinks. The basic work surface might either be within a white or neutral spectrum, using limestone, laminate or pale-toned Corian (not ceramic tiles as they are difficult to keep clean and can crack). Otherwise, choose a surface that contrasts with the white – treated and sealed wood, slate or dark-toned marble, or a brightly coloured resin. Behind the working surface, hob and sink tiles are traditional but glass – frosted or clear – metal, slate, marble and stone are also options.

Cabinet fronts and base units can have doors of solid wood or – more usually – fronts that are either laminated, faced with metal or finished with wood veneers. In the white kitchen, as in any other, too many doors of the same material makes a room heavy and boring, and it is wise to break them

ABOVE White should always be uncluttered and simple; here the hob slides into its own recess when no longer needed.

ABOVE RIGHT This kitchen comfortably looks as if it has always been there, with its white painted wood units and old tiled floor.

OPPOSITE A white kitchen can be as much about entertaining and the enjoyment of food as it is about preparation.

up either with open shelving or glass-fronted doors. The sink can be anything from shiny stainless steel to a traditional deep ceramic Belfast model, or even a smoothly moulded synthetic.

DINING STYLES

If the kitchen is also where you eat, harmonize the style of dining table and chairs with the overall theme and mood of the working part of the room, for although it is a good thing to have the idea of eating distinct from that of cooking, there should be some synchronization – a country table and chairs will usually look out of place in a kitchen of chrome and steel, and vice versa. Furnish the food preparation area with pictures and objects that make the room a place of relaxation and pleasure – this is the purpose of every good kitchen, after all.

THIS PAGE A country dining room in which the white crockery is off-set by the use of pumpkins as decoration – two real and one a ceramic copy.

THIS PAGE A table with white china, old and new, as well as white milk glass, set on a white cloth, is immediately welcoming.

Table Settings

- An all-white mis-matched set works best if there is strong contrast between shapes

- A contrast of tones is also beguiling – combine cream earthenware with porcelain.

- All-white china is well served by a tablecloth of a contrasting colour.

- On any all-white table, flowers and other decorative objects come into their own.

One of the most harmonious ways of setting a table is to mix and match the china and glass in what is now often called a harlequin set – and one of the most effective of harlequin sets is that achieved by only using white crockery. It might be pure white, it might be different designs that all feature a white ground, or it might be designs banded in a different colour against a white background. When you use a combination of plates, serving dishes and bowls in slightly different glazes and designs, each piece is made much more of, and it is easy to appreciate the subtle differences between each pattern and design. It is an effective way to combine old and new, as well as the expensive and less so – many a harlequin set is formed on finds from the junk shop.

ABOVE White china and brown-tinted glass on a dark wooden surface gives an easy-to-achieve look of effortless sophistication.

RIGHT Shape is very important: the decorative lilies echo both the flute-shaped glasses and the white-glazed bowls.

HALLS, STAIRWAYS
AND CORRIDORS

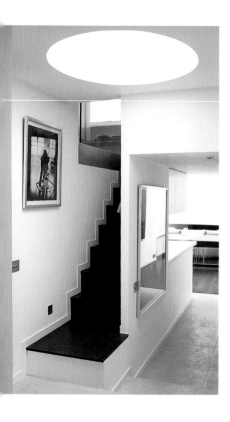

In a predominantly white- painted interior, the dark staircase is a strong and graphic contrast, leading dramatically up to the upper floor.

It is well known that blocks of strong colour break up a space as solidly and as definitely as a closed door; the opposite also applies – a single, light-reflecting colour used over a space will effectively free it, opening it up and encouraging a flow of purpose and function. And, of course, no colour does this better than white, with its light reflective qualities and its ability to expand space and blur boundaries, as well as adding depth and height. The advantages therefore of using a white-based scheme for halls and staircases, as well as in any connecting corridors, are immediately obvious, and broad in their scope, particularly since in many ways these conduits between rooms are in some ways the most important spaces of all.

The hall has changed over the last 800 years from being the principal room in a house, where the household congregated, ate and slept, to being today, with but a few exceptions, merely an introduction to the house itself, often nothing more than a lobby. But it is important to remember that any hall, no matter how small, and how much a shadow of its once-imposing self, is still a very important part of the whole – some might say, the most important part, certainly as far as first impressions are concerned. A hall says a lot about the inhabitants of the house or apartment; it also gives, whether you like it or not, the first impression to a visitor, not only of the spaces beyond but also of your personality and what they might expect. If the space is cold and unwelcoming – then, well, work it out . . ! If, on the other hand, the hall seems friendly and warm, the welcome beyond will seem assured.

Occasionally, a hall is much more than a superannuated lobby, almost a small (or even large) room in its own right; if you have the fortune to have such a room, use it as such – add a comfortable chair, a small table and objects and pictures to stimulate and excite. It can immediately raise the spirits to have something interesting to look at the moment you enter a house or

THIS PAGE A white-limed floor abuts a white-painted staircase with a painted runner that echoes the muted colour of the walls.

apartment — it can even appear to almost become a gallery in miniature, with pictures, objects and even textiles shown against a light, well-lit background.

The staircase is a much underrated design element, but unless it is of exceptional design — a virtuoso piece of contemporary architecture or a rare antique set of stairs and balustrades — it is likely that you may not have actually ever looked at it closely. For most people, the staircase is just another pedestrian objectin the home — a necessary, practical set of steps that lead from one level to another. But to make the most of a

staircase, however small or simple, it is important to look dispassionately at its lines and design, giving thought on how to best give it identity and style in design terms. It's not difficult — even the most unprepossessing set of stairs can be brought into the limelight with the right colours and materials.

Both the hall and the stairs — as well as any central corridors — should be considered, in decorative terms, as a whole, and in the white home that means looking at an overall colour scheme that will give a sense of harmony to what might otherwise be a bit of an

architectural mess. This certainly means a scheme largely based on white tones, enlivened with judicious contrasting tones at various points, encompassing some of the vertical lines of the stairs and the banisters, perhaps, as well as possibly the skirting boards and door frames for a more encompassing look. Depending on the amount of natural light the space receives, the contrast colours that you use might be sharp (citruses, blue-reds or greens); warm (creams and buttermilk, mixed with soft pinks and terracottas); or cool (bright white combined with black, grey and metallic finishes).

Halls, staircases and corridors should, of course, be as well lit as possible, for safety resons as well as for aesthetic considerations, through the carefully considered use of both natural and artificial lighting; even if the space is filled with natural light during the day you will need efficient directional lighting as well as a degree of ambient lighting to create an impression of warmth and welcome. Position the directional light with care, taking into account any potential blind or hazardous spots for anyone entering the space, particularly on the lower reaches of the staircase.

THIS PAGE An all-white corridor is lit both from above and below, with corresponding panels set both into the floor and the ceiling.

Bringing Light into Hallways

- To increase the flow of natural light insert a panel of glass bricks into a wall.

- Treads and risers of stairs should be easily visible – try small lights at floor level.

- A soft effect is obtained by using off-whites on surfaces with well-placed lighting.

- Don't ignore the floor – cover it with high-gloss white paint.

The solitary naked bulb lighting a drab passage is not often seen today, but too often little thought is given to how to light transitory areas in a way that is both practical and attractive. With some judicious use of light-reflective materials and surfaces, or by opening up the space with the use of glass inserts or internal windows, you can give atmosphere and interest to what is often a rather dull space. Choose light-reflective shades of white on the walls that will work with carefully placed lighting to give a feeling of space. Italian polished plaster is an ideal material; its deep sheen will bring light to even the darkest corners. Think laterally: cleverly placed mirrors will maximize the impact of artificial light and make the best use of any natural light that is available.

ABOVE An empty corridor is transformed into a mini gallery for displaying artwork and flowers in a light-filled, airy space.

RIGHT An open-sided staircase, an internal window and white materials on every surface: a recipe for light.

PEACEFUL BEDROOMS

In no other room is white more popular

than in the bedroom, and no wonder – white does after all symbolize peace and calm, and it is the colour of sanctuary. Where better to enjoy such qualities than in the bedroom? For all those reasons, a successful white bedroom should, in principle, be the easiest of all concepts to achieve, but, in fact, to decorate a white bedroom that really works requires just as much – if not more – thought than any other room in the house.

The tone or tones of the background white in a bedroom require a deal of thought: brilliant, bright whites are possibly too unforgiving for a room that should be designed to soothe, and can look unwelcomingly stark – quite the

ABOVE LEFT Under the eaves, white walls and a low white bed with a folding wooden stool as a bedside table create an atmosphere that is both feminine and cosy.

LEFT In an attic room a painted white-gloss floor, and a tall fabric-covered headboard fill and maximize the small space.

RIGHT A white bedroom allows space for decorative, even fanciful, detail, such as an elaborate chandelier and beaded lamp.

LEFT In a loft-style flat, the bed is separated from the sitting area by a partition and light-giving glass doors.

BELOW LEFT In a beamed attic, a white floor and low-level bed dressed in white make good use of space.

RIGHT A sliding door hides storage, leaving space around the white bed.

BELOW RIGHT In a Manhattan loft, the bed is set at an angle, against a wall that hides storage.

BELOW FAR RIGHT White walls and woodwork allow the windows to frame the natural art outside.

opposite from the required effect. Better to look at the palette of creamy whites – buttermilk, parchment, cream – tones which give warmth while retaining their neutral status. Again, two or three shades of these whites used together gives a much deeper, more satisfying appearance than one shade alone, particularly when the woodwork is coloured in such a way that an imperceptible difference can be seen between it and the colour of the walls. Accents of contrast colour are fine, of course, but, on the whole, the bedroom is not the place for making your most challenging colour statements. Not only is it a room generally used to relax in, it is also where you wake up and the space to which you retreat in times of illness.

USING FABRICS IN THE BEDROOM

Textiles make up a large part of a bedroom, and while white makes the most feminine (as well as the most masculine) of bedrooms, it is important to remember that feminine is not at all the same thing as fussy or frilly. The perfect white bedroom does not include frill-edged sheets and pillowcases, ruffle-bedecked curtains and full floor-length table covers. On the bed there

might be white bed linen – popular again, (although for many it never went away) and far more conducive to the feeling of all-pervasive peace that is an element of the best bedrooms. Perhaps the linen will be partially decorated, but it will still be predominantly white and it will always look crisp, clean and pressed; on that point, if white is the theme of the bedroom, all the white textiles within it, from the curtains to the sheets – and in particular the bed cover – must always be maintained in its original pristine state; any hint of grime or grub instantly nullifies the desired effect.

CLEAN, UNFUSSY LINES

Second only to a pristine appearance – or actually part of the same design equation – is relative simplicity of line, another important factor in the successful white bedroom. This particularly applies to any window and bed hangings; ornate or elaborate styles do not really work well in a bedroom. Save them – if you must – for more formal reception areas. Curtains or blinds are obviously of great importance in the bedroom; they must not only be stylistically complementary to the mood of the room, but they must also keep out any unwanted light and add privacy. Blinds too, accentuate peace

LEFT In this small bedroom, French windows have been dressed with individual white blinds to maximize the space.

THIS PAGE Contrast edging on white linen always makes the white look even whiter.

A WHITE BEDROOM IS THE ULTIMATE ANSWER IN THE ELUSIVE, CONSTANT QUEST FOR PEACE AND QUIET

THIS PAGE There is an
almost tropical look to this
room with its ceiling fan,
white floor and daylight
diffused through blinds.

RIGHT ABOVE A pretty
period window has narrow,
gathered curtains that can
be pulled right back for
maximum effect.

RIGHT BELOW An antique
iron bed, re-painted in
shiny white, is matched by
a commodious white-
painted wooden armoire.

and harmony as well as filtering the daylight. Roller blinds that are made of a semi-opaque material can be used in the day to filter the light, perhaps teamed with drawing curtains; another option increasingly chosen by many city dwellers is to have blinds made in white or coloured black-out material, teamed with either another flat-pleated Roman blind, or dress curtains. If the exclusion of light is not a particular problem, installing Venetian blinds or wooden louvered shutters can give a clean, sharp line without descending into clinical mode.

WINDOW TREATMENTS

Although it seems obvious to say, curtains (and bed hangings) should be designed in harmony with the rest of the room, and if the bed is to be dressed, no matter how simply, the design of the window dressing should be in keeping with that of the bed – not necessarily exactly the same but executed in scale and harmony. The idea of dressing the bed – of hanging curtains of some description round the frame or from a fixed point on the wall or ceiling – was for some time out of favour in the contemporary bedroom, possibly because of remembered associations with heavy, dark wood four-poster beds hung with equally heavy, sound and light absorbing curtains that were often as dusty as they were weighty. But today, the concept of bed hangings is once again in favour, albeit in infinitely simpler mode. Diaphanous cheesecloth or muslin hung on bamboo poles around the bed, antique linen sheets on wall-attached metal rods, or unlined cotton falling from a central corona, large or small, and set above the bed, on the wall or the ceiling, are all ideas that work equally well in the new white bedroom.

FINAL TOUCHES

Although some will settle for no less than comfortable carpet underfoot throughout the bedroom, others prefer the relative freedom of floors that are of made of natural materials and augmented by judiciously placed rugs. Wood, whether polished, limed or painted, is warm underfoot and texturally interesting. Cool stone, marble and terracotta really only work well in warm climates, and then only with addition of rugs placed near the bed – cold floors and cold feet do not make for a peaceful start to the day.

Lighting in any bedroom, but particularly in a white bedroom, must be adaptable, able to give 'front of house' lighting if necessary, but also able to be

ABOVE A four-poster bed
is without bed hangings –
the better to appreciate
its simple, clean lines.

ABOVE RIGHT In a small
room, white walls display a
collection of pictures;
sharp contrast is best.

RIGHT Bookcases either
side make a recess for the
bed and the upholstered
headboard rests against a
handsome piece of
moulded panelling.

soft, relaxing, and altogether peaceful. Reading lights should be tall enough
to shed light onto a book rather than the floor, and on all ambient lighting
dimmer switches are pretty important – some would say, essential.

As in the white sitting room, the white bedroom must hold enough
storage space for everything you wish to keep there; clutter and white are
never a good combination, clutter and chaos being the antithesis of peace and
calm. If you want to have all your clothes and accessories stored within the
bedroom rather than a separate room – the ideal solution – think of using
differently size cupboards and chests that pass as furniture, such as a kitchen
armoire combining shelves and drawers, or an old ornate, but heavy wood
wardrobe that can be painted and decorated to create an object of cheerful
beauty. Curtained or screened areas, open shelves, a selection of baskets and
chests – the options are varied, the solutions many.

Dressing a Bed

- Whatever fabric you choose, use enough of it; it is fullness rather than rarity that makes the impact.

- Make sure that full-length curtains do actually touch the floor; on large beds, the curtains will look better if the bottom actually rests on the floor.

- Keep additional decorative touches to a minimum; too many trimmings, such as fringing, tassels, ruffles and frills, will detract rather than enhance

Although we no longer need to dress our beds with curtains for privacy and warmth – which were, of course, the original very practical reasons for such apparent flamboyance – the idea of draping fabric around a bed is still very appealing and relatively easy to achieve. Heavy hangings no longer look right – a light touch is more contemporary. If your bed has a frame, try floor-length curtains of unlined muslin, raw or lining silk, or unmatched old linen sheets. There is no need to hang curtains at every corner, just the head of the bed will do, and there is no need for them to draw; it is the effect rather than the actuality you are looking for. Other relatively easy attainable styles include a corona or coronet – a half circle frame attached to the ceiling or the wall behind the bed, with fabric draped from it down the sides of the bed – and a canopy, which can be as simple as a decorative piece of old or new material draped over rods at the head of the bed. When dressing your bed remember to take into account the design and style of any window curtains. A sympathetic harmony between window and bed is essential.

LEFT In a French bedroom, heavy antique linen sheets are draped on narrow rods round the bed.

RIGHT A period wooden canopy with a matching, equally decorative headboard is richly hung in traditional manner.

FAR RIGHT The entire bedroom is generously hung with white muslin which, around the bed, is softly pleated, draped and caught back at the sides.

LEFT Gently diffused light floods this peaceful, small bathroom, where the bath tub has been raised and placed directly beneath the window.

REFRESHING BATHROOMS

No wonder white is so popular as a decorating colour – its versatility is admirable: not only does it evoke peace, quiet and calm, it is also irrevocably associated with cleanliness and freshness – most keenly of course in the all-white bathroom. Thankfully, the days of having aubergine, avocado and mushroom (such mouth-watering names, but such a disappointing reality) bathroom suites are now pretty much gone – until the next retro revival, that is. White is once again in the ascendant.

Apart from any other considerations of taste, this makes life so much easier, in that if white is the ultimate choice of colour, then the basin and bath and lavatory, whatever material they are made from, do not necessarily have to come from the same range, but can be chosen according to whether they

ABOVE The antique, three-sided mirror placed on a marble splashback, directly above a simple white basin, becomes almost a sculptural object.

LEFT A white background
allows you a canvas on
which to stamp your
personal style, as with this
eclectic mix of decoration,
brought together by the
monochromatic scheme.

RIGHT The freestanding
roll-top bath has been
sited immediately beneath
the skylight, which lights
it and the comfortable
armchair in the corner.

fit the particular space allotted to them and whether they suit the bathroom as a whole, as well as your particular practical and aesthetic needs.

SELECTING A STYLE

On the question of aesthetics, there are various directions the white bathroom can follow. For some, happiness is the comfortable, luxurious bathroom, the 21st-century version of the Edwardian country house bathroom, which features, of course, a large sunny room, furnished with oriental rugs and thick Turkish towels in which a deep, brass-tapped, roll-top bath dominates. Not so likely today perhaps, but the roll-top

bath is as popular as ever, and just as inviting, with its suggestion of long lazy soaks in luxuriously scented water; deep fluffy towels are a contemporary bathroom must and a rug is still a welcome addition to a floor.

The country bathroom, complete with tongue-and-groove boarding around the bath, and often on part or all of the walls and ceiling as well, is another white bathroom option and one incidentally that is as at home in a small town bathroom as outside the city. The wood boarding can be painted in soft whites or pastel tones, in as simple a manner as possible, this being the essence of the look. If you have a shower curtain in your bath, make or buy an outer cotton

curtain, that could be made from voile or cotton, and which is hung over the top of the plastic one outside the bath, to give a more authentic country look.

For some the essence of the contemporary white bathroom is one that generates a sense of freshness and wellbeing, inspired by the spa and health club – light and airy with enough room to store and use oils and unguents, salts and scrubs, with a multi-headed shower and possibly, in a large room, an exercise area. One of the easiest ways to keep bottles and pots near to hand, particularly if the bath is ranged along a wall, is to have as deep a surround as possible; it is invaluable for soaps, unguents and a reviving glass of wine or cup of tea. It also architecturally gives the bath room to breathe and can make even the smallest bathroom appear more spacious.

The white bathrooms of the 1920s and '30s went down a different route – all heavy glamour, mirrored glass, chrome taps and fittings, black marble and cool white lighting, with mirrors backlit or edged with strip lighting ; this is

ABOVE AND RIGHT Like an altar, this marble bath stands in front of a window in an all-marble room of pure and simple severity. Nothing intrudes on the aesthetic, not even the bathroom mirrors, which are hidden inside doors that, when closed, are set flush to the wall.

LEFT Rarely seen, but wonderfully inviting, a double- sized shower with twin shower heads as well as a commodious bath.

BELOW A shower in a bedroom with three walls of glass and one of *pate de verre* mosaic, behind which the basin and storage are hidden.

RIGHT A shower without a door, but instead a curved wall, which makes even the smallest of bathrooms seem very spacious.

an enduringly luxurious look, easily replicated today using either original pieces if you can source them or their modern equivalents, and one that is neither too masculine nor too feminine, just timelessly glamorous.

SHOWERS

Shower rooms and, ever increasingly, wet rooms are more and more popular and some of the most successful are designed in white combined with natural elements, such as stone or marble as well as rough or polished plaster or concrete. The design of showers and their surroundings has advanced considerably over the last few years and, providing there is the space, the shower no longer has to be confined to the size of the miserable little tray in

which not even a kitten could be swung. Indeed, there is often no reason to have a shower door at all; many showers are now designed in a more Mediterranean manner, in that the actual unit is approached round a corner or a curving wall. As with the distribution and positioning of storage, keep an open mind on where the shower might go, and how much room it might take.

MATERIALS AND SURFACES

Whatever style or type of bathroom you decide on, this is the place for natural materials and all the variants of white can shine here – stone, marble, tiles. Basins are available now carved out of stone or marble as well as glass and steel, looking more like rock pools, fountains, and sculpted bowls than boring old basins. Place them strategically to show off their beauty, resting them on a surface that complements the materials (and hides the necessary plumbing). White tiles are generally a good thing in a bathroom and the choice is between a high glazed sparkling white finish and a softer glaze like that used by many Italian and French potters which show, subtly, the tones of the terracotta beneath. If your existing bathroom already has tiles which are old, coloured or patterned, and generally not to your liking, they can be painted into sparkling whiteness with a specially formulated tile paint. There are other options, particularly behind the bath and basin: marble and stone are good looking and practical, and a painted or wooden surface can be protected with a high-gloss glaze finish or a glass or Perspex panel.

And once you have made your final choice of all the different elements that will make up the perfect white bathroom, make sure you do not forget the most important fixture in any bathroom, that bringer of comfort through the cold and the damp and the early mornings starts – the heated towel rail.

LEFT ABOVE An unusual walk-around basin is set into a column of Carrara marble, making it a striking feature in its own right.

LEFT BELOW The tiles in this simple but luxurious bathroom are of hand-cut Carrara white marble with a black marble border; the bath and basin are also made of marble.

RIGHT The rough-textured wall is composed of horizontal strips of hand-cut marble; the simple bowl-shaped basin sits on a shelf of wenge wood.

Suppliers

PAINT

ALBANY PAINTS
Albany House
Ashford Road
Eastbourne
East Sussex BN21 3TR
Tel:)1323 411080

AURO ORGANIC PAINTS
Cheltenham Road
Bisley, Stroud
Gloucestershire GL6 7BX
Tel: 01452 772020
www.auro.co.uk

BREWERS
283-85 New North Road
Islington
London N1 7AA
Tel: 020 7226 2569
www.brewers.co.uk

CRAIG & ROSE PAINTS
Unit 8,
Halbeath Industrial Estate
Crossgates Road
Dunfermline
Fife KY11 7EG
Tel: 01383 740011
www.craigandrose.com

CROWN PAINTS
PO Box 37
Crown House
Hollins Road, Darwen
Lancashire BB3 0BG
Tel: 0870 240 1127
www.crownpaint.co.uk

HOLKHAM LINSEED PAINTS
The Clock Tower
Longlands, Holkham
Wells-Next-The-Sea
Norfolk NR23 1RU
Tel: 01328 711348
www.holkham.co.uk/linseedpaints

DESIGNER COLOURS
389-391 Honeypot Lane
Stanmore
Middlesex HA7 1JJ
Tel: 020 8905 0667
www.designercolours.com

www.designerpaint.co.uk
Tel: 01323 430886

DULUX PAINTS
Customer Care Centre
ICI Paints
Wexham Road
Slough SL2 5DS
Tel: 01753 550555
www.dulux.co.uk

FARROW & BALL LTD
Uddens Estate
Wimborne, Dorset
BH21 7NL
United Kingdom
Tel: 01202 876141
www.farrow-ball.com

FIRED EARTH
3 Twyford Mill
Oxford Road, Adderbury
Near Banbury
Oxfordshire OX17 3SX
Tel: 01295 812088
www.firedearth.com

HOLMANS SPECIALIST PAINTS
1 Central Trading Estate
Signal Way, Swindon
Wiltshire SN3 1PD
Tel: 01793-511537
www.holmanpaints.co.uk

THE LITTLE GREENE PAINT
Company Ltd
Wood Street
Openshaw
Manchester M11 2FB
Tel: 0161 230 0880
www.thelittlegreene.com

NORDIC STYLE
109 Lots Road
London SW10 0RN
Tel: 020 7351 1755
www.nordicstyle.com

NUTSHELL NATURAL PAINTS
PO Box 72
South Brent TQ10 9YR
Tel: 08700 331140
www.nutshellpaints.com

THE PAINT LIBRARY
18 Pond Place
London SW3 6QJ
Tel: 020 7823 7755
www.paintlibrary.co.uk

PAPERS AND PAINTS
4 Park Walk
London SW10
Tel: 020 7352 8626

JOHN OLIVER
33 Pembridge Road
London W11 3HG
Tel: 020 7221 6466
www.johnoliver.co.uk

S&A SUPPLIES
258-260 London Road
Westcliff-on-Sea
Essex SS0 7JG
Tel: 01702 433945
www.sandasupplies.co.uk

SANDERSON PAINTS
Sanderson House
Oxford Rd, Denham
Middlesex UB9 4DX
Tel: 01895 830044
www.sanderson-online.co.uk

ZOFFANY
Chalfont House
Oxford Road
Denham UB9 4DX
Tel: 08708 300 350
www.zoffany.co.uk

FABRIC

ANNIE'S VINTAGE COSTUME
AND TEXTILES
10 Camden Passage
London N1 8EG
Tel: 020 7359 0796

BAER & INGRAM
Tel: 01373 813800
www.baer-ingram.co.uk

BENNETT SILKS
Crown Royal Park
Higher Hillgate
Stockport SK1 3HB
Tel: 0161 476 8600
www.bennett-silks.co.uk

CARDEN CUNIETTI
83 Westbourne Park Road
London W2 5QH
Tel: 020 7229 8559
www.carden-cunietti.com

JANE CHURCHILL
151 Sloane Street
London SW1X 9BX
Tel: 020 7730 9847
www.janechurchill.com

CINNABAR FABRICS
9 Blane Avenue
Blanefield
Glasgow G63 9HU
Tel: 01360 771980
www.cinnabarfabrics.com

AGNÈS COMAR
Paris, France
Tel: +33.4.952.0167
Infodesign@agnescomar.com

CROWSON FABRICS
Crowson House
Bellbrook Park
Uckfield
East Sussex TN22 1QZ
Tel: 01825 761055
www.crowsonfabrics.com

GRAHAM AND GREEN
4 Elgin Crescent
London W11 2JA
Tel: 020 7727 4594

JUDY GREENWOOD ANTIQUES
657 Fulham Road
London SW6 5PY
Tel: 020 7736 6037

GURR AND SPRAKE
283 Lillie Road
London SW6 7LL
Tel: 020 7736 4638

HARLEQUIN
HJH Showroom
Chelsea Harbour
London SW10 0XE
Tel: 08708 300032
www.harlequin.uk.com

KELLY HOPPEN
2 Munden Street
London W14 0RH
Tel: 020 7471 3350
www.kellyhoppen.com

KNICKERBEAN
4 Out Northgate Street
Bury St. Edmunds
Suffolk IP33 1JQ
Tel: 01284 704055
www.knickerbean.com

LOW WOODS FURNISHINGS
Low Woods Lane, Belton
Nr Loughborough
Leicestershire LE12 9TR
Tel: 01530 222246
www.lowwoodsfurnishings.co.uk

IAN MANKIN
109 Regents Park Road
London NW1 8UR
Tel: 020 7722 0997

MONKWELL FABRICS
227 Kings Road
London SW3 5EJ
Tel: 01825 747 903
www.monkwell.com

QUEENSHILL
South Lodge
Queens Hill, Ascot
Berkshire SL5 7EG
Tel: 01344 875419
www.queenshill.com

ROMO LIMITED
Lowmoor Road
Kirkby in Ashfield
Nottinghamshire NG17 7DE
Tel: 01623 756699
www.romofabrics.com

VV ROULEAUX
54 Sloane Square
London SW1 8AX
Tel: 020 7730 3125
www.vvrouleaux.com

GEORGE SPENCER DESIGNS
33 Elystan Street
London SW3 3NT
Tel: 020 7584 3003
www.georgespencer.com

TODAY INTERIORS
Hollis Road, Grantham
Lincolnshire NG31 7QH
Tel: 01476 574401
www.today-interiors.co.uk/

WHALEYS (BRADFORD)
LIMITED
Harris Court
Great Horton
Bradford
West Yorkshire BD7 4EQ
Tel: 01274 576718
www.whaleys-bradford.ltd.uk

WARWICK FABRICS (UK) LTD
Hackling House
Bourton Industrial Park
Bourton-on-the-water
Gloucestershire GL54 2HQ
Tel: 01451 822383
www.warwick.co.uk

WILMAN INTERIORS
CWV Group Ltd
Heasandford Industrial
Estate
Widow Hill Road, Burnley
Lancashire BB10 2TJ
Tel: 01282 727300
www.wilman.co.uk

CURTAIN DESIGNERS & MAKERS

BERY DESIGNS
London
Tel: 020 7924 2197
www.berydesigns.com

STUART HANDS
(curtain maker)
London
Tel: 020 7373 0068

JACQUELYNNE P LANHAM
Designs Inc
Atlanta
Georgia
USA
Tel: +1.404.364.0472

BED LINEN

AND SO TO BED
Tel: 0808 144 4343
www.andsotobed.co.uk

ANTIQUE DESIGNS LTD
Ash House, Ash House Lane
Little Leigh, Northwich
Cheshire CW8 4RG
Tel: 01606 892822/3
www.antique-designs.co.uk

COLOGNE & COTTON LTD
74 Regent Street
Royal Leamington Spa
Warwickshire CV32 4NS
Tel: 0 1926 881485
www.cologneandcotton.net

DAMASK
10 Sullivan Enterprise Centre
Sullivan Road
London SW6 3DJ
Tel: 020 7384 2358
www.damask.co.uk

THE EGYPTIAN COTTON
STORE LTD
76 Ewhurst Road, Crawley
West Sussex RH11 7HE
Tel: 0845 226 0098
www.egyptiancottonstore.com

GIVAN'S IRISH LINEN
Suite14, Queen Street
Chambers
Queen Street
Peterborough PE1 1PA
Tel: 01733 562 300
www.givans.co.uk

JOHN LEWIS
Oxford Street
London W1A 1EX
Tel: 020 7629 7711
www.johnlewis.com

KING OF COTTON
Unit 5, The Sandycombe
Centre
1/9 Sandycombe Road
Richmond on Thames
Surrey TW9 2EP
Tel: 020 8332 7999
www.kingofcotton.co.uk

PAVILION TEXTILES
Freshford Hall
Freshford
Bath BA3 6EJ
Tel: 01225 722522

PETER REED LTD
1 Farrington Place
Burnley
Lancashire BB11 5TY
Tel: 01282 832 515
www.peter-reed.com

JANE SACCHI LINENS LTD
Worlds End Studios
132-34 Lots Road
London SW10 0RJ
Tel: 020 7349 7020
www.janesacchi.com

SILKWOOD SILK LTD
Standing Hill
Minety
Malmesbury
Wiltshire SN16 9RH
Tel: 01666 860003
www.silkwoodsilk.com

TOBIAS AND THE ANGEL
68 Whitehart Lane
Barnes
London SW13 0PZ
Tel: 020 8878 8902

TONDER & TONDER
Bryants Farm
Dunsden
Berkshire RG4 9PB
Tel: 0118 946 3704
www.tonderandtonder.co.uk

VOLGA LINEN COMPANY
Unit 1A, Eastlands Road
Industrial Estate
Leiston
Suffolk IP16 4LL
Tel: 01728 635 020
www.volgalinen.co.uk

THE WHITE COMPANY
Tel: 0870 900 9555
www.thewhitecompany.com

THE WHITE HOUSE
102 Waterford
London SW6 2HA
Tel: 020 7629 3521
www.the-white-house.com

WOODS OF HARROGATE
LIMITED
Prince Albert Row
65/67 Station Parade
Harrogate
North Yorkshire HG1 1ST
Tel: 01423 530111
www.woodsofharrogate.co.uk

CHINA

ALWAYS PORCELAIN LIMITED
c/o Moss Lodge Fish Farm
Moss Road, Moss
Doncaster
South Yorkshire DN6 OHF
Tel: 01302 700959
www.alwaysporcelain.com

BELLEEK POTTERY
Tel: 0028 6865 9314
www.belleek.com

BRANKSOME CHINA
Shaftesbury St
Fordingbridge
Hampshire SP6 1JF
Tel: 01425 652010

CHINACRAFT LTD
Parke House
130 Barlby Road
London W10 6BW
Tel: 020 7565 5876
www.chinacraft .co.uk

THE COOKING SHOP
Jules Brinton Ltd
Unit 8A, Churchfields
Business Park
Clensmore Street
Kidderminster
Worcestershire DY10 2JY
Tel: 01562 510440
www.thecookingshop.com

THE CROCKERY BARN
Ashbocking, Ipswich
Suffolk IP6 9JS
Tel: 01473-890123
www.thecrockerybarn.co.uk

THE DENBY POTTERY
COMPANY
Denby
Derbyshire DE5 8NX
Tel: 01773 740899
www.denbypottery.co.uk

DIBOR
20a West Park
Harrrogate
North Yorkshire HG1 1BJ
Tel: 0870 0133 666
www.dibor.co.uk

DIVERTIMENTI
139-41 Fulham Road
London SW3 6SD
Tel: 020 7581 8065
www.divertimenti.co.uk

ESSENTIALLY WHITE LIMITED
1 Ford Place Cottages
Ford Lane, Wrotham Heath
Sevenoaks
Kent TN15 7SE
Tel: 0845 404 9505
www.essentiallywhite.co.uk

THE GENERAL TRADING
COMPANY
2 Symons Street
Sloane Square
London SW3 2TJ
Tel: 020 7730 0411
www.general-trading.co.uk

THOMAS GOODE & CO
19 South Audley Street
London W1K 2BN
Tel: 020 7499 2823
www.thomasgoode.com

R HAVENS LTD
138/140 Hamlet Court Road
Westcliff-on-Sea
Essex SSO 7LW
Tel: 01702 342757
www.havens.co.uk

MARKS AND SPENCER
GROUP PLC
Waterside House
35 North Wharf Road
London W2 1NW
Tel: 020 7935 4422
www.marksandspencer.com

DAVID MELLOR
4 Sloane Square
Lodnon SW1 8EE
Tel: 020 7730 4259

OKA DIRECT
Chene Court, Poundwell
Street
Modbury
Devon PL21 0QL
Tel: 0870 160 6002
www.okadirect.com

REJECT CHINA SHOP
183 Brompton Road
London SW3 1NF
Tel: 020 7581 0739

ROYAL CREAMWARE FINE
CHINA
Royal Chintz
Wolrld Wide Shopping Mall Ltd
Chancery Lane, Malton
North Yorkshire YO17 7HW
Tel: 01653 602880
www.royalcreamware.co.uk

ROYAL DOULTON PLC
Sir Henry Doulton House
Forge Lane, Etruria
Stoke-on-Trrent
Staffordshire ST1 5NN
Tel: 01782 404045
www.royal-doulton.com

ROYAL WORCESTER
Severn Street
Worcester WR1 2NE
Tel: 01905 23221
www.royal-worcester.co.uk

SMALL ISLAND TRADER LTD
Brockton Hall
Brockton
Stafffordshire ST21 6LY
Tel: 01785 851800
www.smallislandtrader.com

SPODE
Church Street
Stoke-on-Trent
Staffordshire ST4 1BX
Tel: 01782 744011
www.spode.co.uk

TABLEWARE UK
183 Brompton Road
London SW3 1NF
Tel: 020 7565 5883
www.tableware.uk.com

JOSIAH WEDGWOOD &
SONS LTD
Barlaston
Stoke-on-Trent
Staffordshire ST12 9ES
Tel: 01782 204141
www.wedgwood.com

VILLEROY & BOCH
267 Merton Road
London SW18 5JS
Tel: 020 8871 0011
eshop.villeroy-boch.com/uk

CARPETS AND RUGS

AVENA CARPETS
Bankfields Mill
Haley Hill, Halifax
West Yorkshire HX3 6ED
Tel: 01422 330261
www.avena-carpets.com

BRINTONS CARPETS
Tel: 0800 505055
www.brintons.net

www.carpetinfo.co.uk
Carpet manufactuers and
suppliers in the UK

CRUCIAL TRADING
The Plaza
535 Kings Road
London SW10
Tel: 020 7376 7100
www.crucial-trading.com

CHRISTOPHER FARR
6 Burnstall Street
London SW3 3ZJ
Tel: 020 7349 0888
www.cfarr.co.uk

ROGER OATES
1 Munro Terrace
Cheyne Walk
London SW10 ODL
Tel: 020 7351 2288
www.rogeroates.com

THE RUG COMPANY
124 Holland Park Avenue
London W11 4UE
Tel: 020 7229 5148
www.therugcompany.org

SINCLAIR TILL
793 Wandsworth Bridge Road
London SW8 3JQ
Tel: 020 7720 0031
www.sinclairtill.co.uk

ROBERT STEPHENSON
1 Eyston Street
Chelsea Green
London SW3 3NT
Tel: 020 7225 2343

WOOL CLASSICS
Chelsea Harbour Design
Centre
Chelsea Harbour
London SW10
Tel: 020 7379 0090

TILES

DOMUS TILES
1 Canterbury Court
6 Camberwell New Road
London SE5
Tel: 0845 062 5555
www.doustiles.com

FIRED EARTH
See PAINT

ISLAND STONE
Postal Address:
78 York Street
London W1H 1DP
Tel: 0800 083 9351
www.islandstone.co.uk

PARIS CERAMICS
583 Kings Road
London SW6 2EH
Tel: 020 7371 7778

PILKINGTON PLC
Prescot Road
St Helens
Merseyside WA10 3TT
Tel: 01744 28882
www.pilkington.co.uk

PORCELANOSA
Marshall House
468-72 Purley Way
Croydon CR0 4RG
Tel: 020-8680 1123
For branches: 0800-915 4000
www.porcelanosa.co.uk

REED HARRIS TILES
Riverside House
27 Carnwath Road
London SW6 3HR
Tel: 020 8877 9774
www.reedharris.co.uk

ROVIC TILES
Unit E4, Chaucer Business
Park
Watery Lane, Kemsing
Sevenoaks
Kent TN15 6YP
Tel: 01732 763167
www.rovic.co.uk

THE STONE & CERAMIC
Warehouse
51/55 Stirling Road
London W3 8DJ
Tel: 020-8993 5545
www.stoneandceramicwareh
ouse.co.uk

STONEHOUSE TILES
42 Enterprise Business Estate
Bolina Road
London SE16 3LF
Tel: 020 7237 5375
Freephone: 0800 0939 724
www.stonehousetiles.co.uk

TAYLOR TILES
The Taylor Group of
Companies
Beaufort Road, Plasmarl
Swansea SA6 8JG
Tel: 01792 797712
www.taylortiles.co.uk

TOPPS TILES
Rushworth House
Handforth, Wilmslow
Cheshire SK9 3HJ
Tel: 0800 783 6262
www.toppstiles.co.uk

WORLD'S END TILES
British Rail Yard
Silverthorne Road
Battersea
London SW8 3HE
Tel: 020 7819 2100
www.worldsendtiles.co.uk

SURFACES

FORMICA LTD UK
Coast Road
North Shields
Tyne and Wear NE29 8RE
Tel: 0191 259 3000
www.formica.co.uk

DALSOUPLE
PO Box 140
Bridgwater
Somerset TA5 1HT
Tel: 01278 727 733
www.dalsouple.com

ABET LAMINATES
70 Roding Road
London Induscrial Park
London E6 4LS
Tel: 020 7473 6910
www.abetlaminati.it

CORIAN
Dupont Corian
Maylands Avenue
Hemel Hempstead
Hertfordshire HP2 7DP
Tel: 0800 962 116
www.corian.com

FIRST FLOOR
174 Wandsworth Bridge Road
London SW6 2UQ
Tel: 020 7736 1123
www.firstfloor.uk.com

STONE AGE
Unit 3
Parsons Green Depot
Parsons Green Lane
London SW6 4HH
Tel: 020 7384 9090
wwwstone-age.co.uk

UK MARBLE LTD
21 Nurcott Road
Hereford HR4 9LW
Tel: 01432 352178
www.ukmarble.co.uk

**LIGHTING AND
ACCESSORIES**

AFTER NOAH
121 Upper Street
London N1 1QP
Tel: 020 7359 4281
www.afternoah.com

ALFIES' ANTIQUE MARKET
13-25 Church Street
London NW8 8DT
Tel: 020 7723 6066
www.alfiesantiques.com

ARTEMIDE
90-92 Great Portland Street
London W1 7JY
Tel: 020 7637 7238
www.artemide.com

LAURA ASHLEY LTD
Freepost SY1225
P.O. Box 19
Newtown
Powys SY16 1DZ
Tel: 0871 9835 999
www.lauraashley.com

BELLA FIGURA
G5 Chelsea Harbour Design
Centre
Chelsea Harbour
London SW10 0XE
Tel: 020 7376 4564
www.bella-figure.co.uk

DAVID CANEPA LIGHTING
Dragonworks
Leigh-on-Mendip
Radstock BA3 5QZ
Tel: 01373 813600
www.canepalighting.co.uk

JOHN CULLEN LIGHTING
585 Kings Road
London SW6 2EH
Tel: 020 7371 5400
www.johncullenlighting.co.uk

DE LE CUONA LTD
9/10 Osborne Mews
Windsor, Berkshire SL4 3DE
Tel: 01753 830301
www.delecuona.co.uk

ERCO
38 Dover Street
London W1
Tel: 020 7408 0320
www.erco.com

HECTOR FINCH
88-90 Wandsworth Bridge
Road
London SW6 2TF
Tel: 020 7731 8886
www.hectorfinch.com

HABITAT
196 Tottenham Court Road
London W1P 9LD
Tel: 0845 601 0740
www.habitat.net

IKEA FURNISHINGS
Brent Park
2 Drury Way
Norht Circular Road
London Nw10 0TH
Tel: 020 8208 5600
www.ikea.com

INHOUSE
24-26 Wilson Street
Glagow G1 1SS
Tel: 0141 552 5902
www.inhouse-uk.com

THE LONDON LIGHTING
COMPANY
135 Fulham Road
London SW3 6RT
Tel: 020 7589 3612

MR LIGHT
279 King's Road
London SW3 5EW
Tel: 020 7352 8398
www.mrlight.co.uk

SKK
34 Lexington Street
London W1F 0LH
Tel: 020 7434 4095
www.skk.net

SCP
135-39 Curtain Road
London EC2A 3BX
Tel: 020 7739 1869
www.scp.co.uk

KITCHENS

AGA RAYBURN
PO Box 30
Ketley
Telford TF1 4DD
Tel: 01952 642000
www.aga-web.co.uk

ALESSI
22 Brook Street
London W1K 5DF
Tel: 020 7518 9091
www.alessi.com

THE ALNO STORE
Halcyon Interiors
120 Wigmore Street
London W1U 3RU
Tel: 020 7486 3080
www.alno.co.uk

ALTERNATIVE PLANS
9 Hester Road
London SW11 4AN
Tel: 020 7228 6460
www.alternative-plans.co.uk

BULTHAUP UK LTD
37 Wigmore Street
London W1
Tel: 020 7495 3663
www.bulthaup.com

JOHNSON & JOHNSON
12-19 Guiness Road
Trading Estate
Trafford Park
Manchester M17 1SB
Tel: 0161 872 7041

POGGENPOHL
Tel: 0800 298 1098
www.poggenpohl.co.uk

JOHN LEWIS OF
HUNGERFORD
156-58 Wandsworth
Bridge Road
Fulham
London SW6 2UH
Tel: 020 7371 5603
www.john-lewis.co.uk

KITCHEN IDEAS
70 Westbourne Grove
London W2 5SH
Tel: 020 7229 3388

MOBEN
12/14 Baker Street
London W1U 3BU
Tel: 0207 935 3406
www.moben.co.uk

NOW GROUP PLC
Red Scar Business Park
Preston PR2 5NA
Tel: 01772 703838
www.nowkitchens.co.uk

SIEMATIC
Ospray House, Rookery Court
Primett Road, Stevenage
Herfordshire SG1 3EE
Tel: 01438 369327

SMALLBONE OF DEVIZES
220 Brompton Road
London SW3 2BB
Tel: 020 7581 9989
www.smallbone.co.uk

BATHROOMS

AQUALISA PRODUCTS
Tel: 01959 560000
www.aqualisa.co.uk

ALTERNATIVE PLANS
See Kitchens

ARMITAGE SHANKS
Armitage, Near Rugby
Staffordshire WS15 4BT
Tel: 01543 490253

ASTON MATTHEWS
141-47a Essex Road
London N1 2SN
Tel: 020 7226 3657
www.astonmatthews.co.uk

BATHROOMS INTERNATIONAL
4 Pont Street
London SW1
Tel: 020 7838 7788
www.bathroomsint.com

BATHSTORE.COM
410-14 Upper Richmond
Road West
London SW14 7JX
Tel: 020 8878 2727
www.bathstore.com

COLOURWASH
63-65 Fulham High Street
London SW6 3JJ
Tel: 020 7371 0911
www.colourwash.co.uk

CZECH & SPEAKE
39c Jermyn Street
London SW1Y 6DN
Tel: 020 7439 0216
www.czechspeake.co.uk

EDWINS
17, 19 & 26 All Saints Road
London W11 1HE
Tel: 020 7221 3550

IDEAL STANDARD
The Bathroom Works
National Avenue
Kingston Upon Hull HU5 4HS
Tel: 01482 346461
www.ideal-standard.co.uk

CP HART & SONS
Newnham Terrace
Hercules Road
London SE1 7DR
Tel: 020 7902 1000
www.cphart.co.uk

ORIGINAL BATHROOMS
143-45 Kew Road
Richmond-upon-Thames
Surrey TW9 2PN
Tel: 020 8940 7554
www.original-bathrooms.co.uk

ROCA LTD
Samson Road
Hermitage Industrial Estate
Coalville
Leicestershire LE67 3FP
Tel: 01530 830080
www.roca-uk.com

TEUCO
Suite 314
Business Design Centre
52 Upper Street
London N1 0QH
Tel: 020 7704 2190
www.teuco.co.uk

TWYFORD BATHROOMS
Lawton Road
Alsager
Stoke on Trent ST7 2DF
Tel: 01270 879777
www.twyfordbathrooms.com

THE WATER MONOPOLY
18-18 Lonsdale Road
London NW6 6RD
Tel: 020 7624 2636
www.watermonopoly.com

WEST ONE BATHROOMS
45-46 South Audley Street
London W1
Tel: 020 7499 1845
www.westonebathrooms.com

VILLEROY & BOCH
See China

STORAGE

IKEA
See Lighting

CHARLES PAGE
61 Fairfax Road
London NW6 4EE
Tel: 020 7328 9875
www.charlespage.co.uk

THE HOLDING COMPANY
241-45 Kings Road
London SW3 5EL
Tel: 020 7352 1600
www.theholdingcompany.co.uk

DOMINIC ASH
Tel: 020 7689 0676
wwwdominiccash.co.uk
Bespoke joinery

MUJI
187 Oxford Street
London W1
Tel: 020 7323 2208 for
branches
www.muji.co.uk

FURNITURE

ARAM DESIGNS
110 Drury Lane
London WC2B 5SG
Tel: 020 7557 7557
www.aram.co.uk

DAVID CHAMPION
199 Westbourne Grove
London W11 2SB
Tel: 020 7727 6016

DECORATIVE LIVING
55 New King's Road
London SW6 4SE
Tel: 020 7736 5623
www.decorativeliving.co.uk

CHAPLINS
477-507 Uxbridge Road
Pinner
Middlesex HA5 4JS
Tel: 020 8421 1779
www.chaplins.co.uk

THE CONRAN SHOP
Michelin House
81 Fulham Road
London SW3 6RD
Tel: 020 7589 7401
www.conran.com

THE DINING CHAIR COMPANY
4 St Barnabus Street
London SW1V 8PE
Tel: 0207259 0422
www.diningchair.co.uk

THE DINING ROOM SHOP
62-64 Whitehart Lane
Barnes
London SW13 0PZ
Tel: 020 8878 1020
www.thediningroomshop.co.uk

GRAND ILLUSIONS
2/4 Crown Road
St Margarets
Twickenham TW1 3EE
Tel: 020 8607 9446
www.grand-illusions.com

HABITAT
See Lighting

HEAL'S
196 Tottenham Court Road
London W1P 9LD
Tel: 020 7636 1666
www.heals.co.uk

JOHN LEWIS
See Bed Linen

KINGCOME SOFAS
304 Fulham Road
London SW10 9EP
Tel: 020 7351 3998

LINUM FRANCE
Z1 La Grande Marine
84800 Isle sur la Sourge
France
Tel: +33.4.90.383.738

LOTS ROAD AUCTION
GALLERIES
71-73 Lots Road
Chelsea SW10
Tel: 020 7351 7771

MARK MAYNARD ANTIQUES
651 Fulham Road
London SW6 5PU
Tel: 020 7731 3533
www.markmaynard.co.uk

NORDIC STYLE
See Paints

LENA PROUDLOCK
25a Long Street
Tetbury
Gloucestershire GL8 8AA
Tel: 01666 500051
www.lenaproudlock.com

PURVES AND PURVES
80-81 Tottenham Court Road
London W1P 9HD
Tel: 020 7580 8223
www.purves.co.uk

Q COLLECTION
Anthony Cochran
915 Broadway
Suite 1001
New York
New York 10010
USA
Tel: +1.212.529.1400
www.qcollection.com

JOSEPHINE RYAN
ANTIQUES
63 Abbeville Road
London SW14 9JW
Tel: 020 8675 3900
www.josephineryanantiques.
co.uk

SKANDIUM
72 Wigmore Street
London W1H 9DL
Tel: 020 7935 2077
www.skandium.com

SOFA WORKSHOP
84 Tottenham Court Road
London W1
Tel: 020 7580 6839
www.sofaworkshopdirect.co.uk

SOLGÅRDEN
Karlavägen 58
114 49 Stockholm
Sweden
Tel: +46.8.663.9360
www.solgarden.net

TIM HOBBY AT SPACE
MODERN DESIGN
800 Peachtree Street NE
Atlanta
Georgia 30308
USA
Tel: +1.404.228.4600
www.spacemodernworld.com

WHITE SENSE
Holländergatan 27
113 59 Stockholm
Sweden
Tel: +46.70.717.5700
www.mezzoshowroom.com

TOBIAS AND THE ANGEL
See Bedlinen

YEOWARD SOUTH
Space S
The Old Imperial Laundry
71 Warriner Gardens
London SW11 4XW
Tel: 020 7351 5454
www.williamyeoward.com

ARCHITECTS

1100 ARCHITECT
435 Hudson Street
New York
New York 10014
USA
Tel: +1.212.645.1011
www.1100architect.com

ATELIER D'ARCHITECTURE
M FRISENNA SCPL
15 rue de Verviers
4020 Liège
Belgium
Tel: +32.4.341.5786

BATAILLE & IBENS DESIGN
NV
Vekestraat 13
Bus 14
2000 Antwerp
Belgium
Tel: +32.2.213.8620
www.bataille-ibens.be

SOLIS BETANCOURT
1739 Connecticut Avenue NW
Washington
DC 20009
USA
Tel+1.202.659.8734
www.solisbetancourt.com

BRUCE BIERMAN DESIGN INC
29th West 15th Street
New York
New York 10011
USA
Tel: +1.212.243.1935
www.biermandesign.com

LAURENT BUTTAZONI
62 rue de Montrueil
75011 Paris
France
Tel: +33.1.40.09.98.49

FRED COLLIN
Bransdale Lodge
York
South Yorkshire YO62 7JL
Tel: 01751 431137

J F DESALLE
3 rue Seguier
75006 Paris
France
Tel: +33.1.43.29.42.76

JAMES GORST
Tel: 020 7336 7140
www.jamesgorstarchitects.com

KOLD
Karl Fournier & Olivier Marty
7 rue Geoffrey l'Angevin
75004 France
Tel: +33.1.42.71.13.92

KARI LALLALAINEN
Tel: +358 9680.1828
Kari.lappalainen@pp7.inet.fi

GENE LEEDY
555 Avenue G NW
Winter Haven
Florida 33880
Tel: +1.863 293 7173
www.geneleedyarchitect.com

JONATHAN LEITERSDORF
Just Design Inc
80 Fifth Avenue
18th Floor
New York
New York 10011
Tel: +1.212.243.6544

MARC PROSMAN
ARCHITECTEN BV
Overtoom 197
1054 HT Amsterdam
The Netherlands
Tel: +31.20.48.92.099
www.prosman.nl

FRANÇOIS MARCQ
8 rue Fernand Neuray
1050 Brussels
Belgium
Tel: +32.2.513.1328

JAMES MOHN DESIGN
Tel: +1.212.414.1477
www.jamesmohndesign.com

GUY PETERSON/OFA INC
1234 First Street
Sarasota
Florida 34236
Tel: +1.941.952.1111
www.guypeterson.com

STEPHEN ROBERTS INC.
Fourth Floor
250 West Broadway
New York
New York 10013
USA
Tel: +1.212.966.6930
www.stephenroberts.com

SHELTON, MINDEL &
ASSOCIATES
143 West 20th Street
New York
New York 10011
USA
Tel: +1.212.243.3939

SMITH CARADOC-HODGKINS
ARCHITECTS
43 Tanner Street
London SW1 3PL
Tel: 020 7407 0717
www.sch-architects.com

STICKLAND COOMBE
ARCHITECTS
258 Lavender Hill
London SW11 1LJ
Tel: 020 7924 1699
www.sticklandcoombe.com

VINCENT VAN DUYSEN
ARCHITECTS
Lomardenvest 34
2000 Antwerp
Belgium
Tel: +32.3.205.9190
www.vincentvanduysen.com

ANDREW WEAVING
Modern@centuryd.com
www.centuryd.com
07808 727615

WELLS MACKERETH
ASSOCIATES
Unit 14 Archer Street Studios
10-11 Archer Street
London W1D 7AZ
Tel: 020 7287 5504
www.wellsmackareth.com

DESIGNERS

ALTERNATIVE PLANS
See Kitchens

TRISTAN AUER
5a Cour de la Métaine
75020 Paris
France
Tel: +33.1.43.49.57.20

DAVID CARTER
109 Mile End Road
London E1 4UJ
Tel: 020 7790 0259
www.alacarter.com

COORENGEL & CALVAGRAC
Design et Decoration
43 rue de l'Echiquier
75010 Paris
France
Tel: +33.1.40.27.14.65

ESCENAS BARCELONA S.L.
13 Pedro de la Creu
08017 Barcelona
Spain
Tel: +34.93.280.3521

FRANK FAULKNER
92 North 5th Street
Hudson
New York 12534
USA
Tel: +1.518.828.2295

SERA HERSHAM LOFTUS
020 7286 5948

KELLY HOPPEN
London
www.kellyhoppen.com

HOLLY HUNT COLLECTION
Furniture & Lighting
801 West Adams
Chicago
Illinois 60607
Tel: +1.312 329 5999
www.hollyhunt.com

INDIGO SEAS
Lynn von Kersting
123 North Robertson
Boulevard
Los Angeles
California 90048
USA
Tel: +1.310.550.8758

CHRISTIAN LIAIGRE LTD
68-70 Fulham Road
London SW3 6HH
Tel: 020 7584 5848
www.christian-liaigre.co.uk

ANGI LINCOLN
07957 621796

FRÉDÉRIC MÉCHICHE
14 rue Saint Croix de la
Bretonnerie
75004 Paris
France
Tel: +33.1.42.78.78.28

PAMPLEMOUSSE DESIGN INC.
Tel: +1.212.980.2033
www.pamplemoussedesign.com

TUULA.POYHONEN@FONET.FI

KRISTIINA RATIA DESIGNS
+1.202.852.0027
kristiinaratia@aol.com

EMMANUEL RENOIRD
4 rue de Phalsbourg
75017 Paris
France
Tel: +33.1.45.56.99.24
www.emmanuelrenoird.com

WILSON STILES INC
83 Cocoanut Avenue
Sarasota
Florida 34236-5613
USA
Tel: +1.941 366 8282

PERI WOLFMAN
148 Green Street, 4E
New York
New York 10012
USA
Tel: +1.212.966.4077

VICENTE WOLF
333 West 39th Street
10th Floor
New York
New York 10018
USA
Tel: +1.212.465.0590

**ANTIQUES, GALLERIES &
SOCIETIES**

FAY GOLD GALLERY
764 Miami Circle
Atlanta
Georgia 30324
USA
Tel: +1.404 233 3843
www.fayfoldgallery.com

LOWE GALLERY
(David Shapiro)
Space A02
75 Bennett Street
Atlanta
Georgia 30309
USA
Tel + 1.404 352 8114
www.lowegallery.com

A.M.S. MARLBOROUGH
Nueva Castanera 3723
Santiago
Chile
Tel: +56 2 228 8696

PLASTER PARAPHERNALIA
Peter Hone
3 Fournier Street
London E1 6QF
Tel: 020 7375 2757

JOSEPHINE RYAN
ANTIQUES & INTERIORS
63 Abbeville Road
London SW4 9JW
Tel: 020 8675 3900
www.josephineryanantiques.
com

SOCIETY FOR THE
PRESERVATION OF NEW
ENGLAND ANTIQUITIES
Harrison Gray Otis House
141 Cambridge Street
Boston
Ma 02114
USA
Tel: +1.617.542.7307
www.spnea.org

MICHAEL TRAPP
7 River Road
Box 67
West Cornwall
Connecticut 06796
USA
Tel: +1.860.672.6098

Acknowledgements

Photographers credits

Ken Hayden 85, 116, 120 left

Simon Upton: 1, 3 left & right, 4, 6 below, 10 right, 12-13, 18-19, 20 above, 22-23, 25 right, 29 above & centre right, below left, 34, 35 left & right, 39, 40-42, 44, 45 below, 46-47, 50-51, 55, 57 above right, 59, 62 right, 63 above left, 64 above, 65-69, 71 left, 72-73, 77 above left, 78-81, 82 above, 83-84, 89 right, 92-93, 96 right, 97 left, 101-108, 112 above, 114 above, 123 left, 125, 126, 127

Frederic Vasseur: 2, 5, 37, 43, 58, 70, 71 right, 77 above right, 109 right, 112 below, 113, 115 above, 119, 120 right, 130 above, 131

Fritz von der Schulenburg: 21, 29 above left, 36 right, 56 below, 57 below right, 115 below left, 123 right

Andrew Wood: Endpapers, 3 centre, 6 above, 7-8, 10 left, 14-18, 20 below, 24, 25 left, 26-27, 29 centre left & below, 30, 31, 32-33, 38, 45 above, 48, 49, 52-54, 56 above & centre, 57 above & below left, 60-61, 62 left, 63 right & below left, 64 below, 66 below left, 74-75, 77 centre & below, 81, 82 below, 86-88, 89 left, 90-92, 94-95, 96 left, 97 right, 98-99, 100 left & right, 108 right, 110-111, 114 below, 115 below right, 116-118, 121, 122, 124, 127-129, 130 below, 132, 134.

Location credits

Prelims: Jasper Conran's home in London.

1 a home featuring Jane Churchill fabrics; 2 Lena Proudlock's house in Gloucestershire; 3 left a home featuring Jane Churchill fabrics; 3 centre an apartment in Brussels designed by Vincent van Duysen; 4 Artists Ben Langlands & Nikki Bell's house in London; 5 Lena Proudlock's house in Gloucestershire; 6 above Sera Hersham Loftus' house in London; 6 below Josephine Ryan's house in London; 7 an apartment in Paris designed by Frédéric Méchiche; 8 an apartment in Brussels designed by Vincent van Duysen; 9 interior by Jacquelynne P Lanham; 10 left Anna Bonde of Linum's house in Provence; 10 right Moussie Sayers of Nordic Style's house in London; 10-11 Fay Gold's home in Atlanta; 12-13 a home featuring Jane Churchill fabrics; 14 Dean Smith & Pearl Wou's home in London; 15 a house in Connecticut designed by Michael Trapp; 16-17 an apartment in Brussels designed by Vincent van Duysen; 17 Surinamplein, Amsterdam, designed by Mark Prosman Archictecten; 18 Susanna Colleoni & Didi Huber's home in Milan; 18-19 Peter Franck & Kathleen Triem's house in Ghent, New York; 20 above artists Ben Langlands & Nikki Bell's house in London; 20 below Susanna Colleoni & Didi Huber's home in Milan; 21 Vicente Wolf's apartment in New York; 22-23 Martine Colliander of White Sense's apartment in Stockholm; 24 Interior by Tuula Poyhonen; 25 left Tristan Auer's apartment in Paris; 25 right Anthony Cochran's apartment in New York; 26-27 a house in the Hampton's designed by Solis Betancourt; 29 above left curtain design by Jacquelynne P Lanham; 29 above right Michael Coorengel and Jean-Pierre Calvagrac's apartment in Paris; 29 centre left Kristiina Ratia's Connecticut home; 29 centre right & below left a home featuring Jane Churchill fabrics; 29 below right an apartment in Belgium designed by François Marcq; 30 above a house in New York designed by Shelton, Mindel and Associates; 30 below left Penthouse loft in New York designed by Bruce Bierman Design Inc.; 30 below right Ralph & Ann Pucci's New York home, furnished in collaboration with Vicente Wolf; 31 Sera Hersham Loftus' house in London; 32 a Penthouse loft in New York designed by Bruce Bierman Design Inc.; 33 Susanna Colleoni & Didi Huber's home in Milan; 36 left Anne Singer's apartment in London; 36 right Curtain maker Stuart Hands, fabric designed by Colleen Bery; 37 Reed & Delphine Krakoff's Manhattan townhouse, designed by Delphine Krakoff of Pamplemousse Design Inc.; 38 Illka apartment in Helsinki, designed by Kari Lappalainen; 39 above left Hank & Debi di Cintio's house in Stockport, New York, designed by Frank Faulkner; 39 below a home featuring Jane Churchill fabrics; 39 right Tim Hobby's apartment in Atlanta, with "Untitled 25" by Todd Murphy from the Lowe Gallery, Atlanta; 40-41 Peter Franck & Kathleen Triem's house in Ghent, New York; 42 above David Carter's house in London; 42 below left Moussie Sayers of Nordic Style's house in London; 42 below right Martin Colliander of White Sense's apartment in Stockholm; 43 Lena Proudlock house in Gloucestershire; 44 Greville & Sophie Worthington's home in Yorkshire; 45 above an apartment in Brussels designed by Vincent van Duysen; 45 below Emmanuel Renoird's house in Normandy; 46-47 a home featuring Jane Churchill fabrics; 48 left Bevan residence, London; 48 right Mr & Mrs van Hool's kitchen designed by Claire Bataille & Paul Ibens Designs; 49 Fred & Helen Collin's house in London; 50-51 a home featuring Jane Churchill fabrics; 51 Anthony Cochran's apartment in New York; 52 Kristiina Ratia's Connecticut home; 53 an apartment in Brussels designed by Vincent van Duysen; 54 Susanna Colleoni & Didi Huber's home in Milan; 55 Jerry & Susan Lauren's apartment in New York; 56 above Nigel Greenwood's apartment in London; 56 centre an apartment in Paris, designed by KOLD; 56 below Curtains designed by Agnès Comar; 57 above left Anna Bonde of Linum's house in Provence; 57 above right a home featuring Jane Churchill fabrics; 57 below left an apartment in Paris designed by Frédéric Méchiche; 57 below right Curtains designed by Kelly Hoppen; 58 left Reed & Delphine Krakoff's Manhattan townhouse, designed by Delphine Krakoff of Pamplemousse Design Inc.; 58 right

Lena Proudlock's house in Gloucestershire; 59 a home featuring Jane Churchill fabrics; 60-61 Sera Hersham Loftus' house in London; 62 left a house in the Hamptons designed by Solis Betancourt; 62 right & 63 above left a home featuring Jane Churchill fabrics; 63 below left Lynn von Kersting's home in Los Angeles; 63 right Laurence Ambrose's house in Provence; 64 above a home featuring Jane Churchill fabrics; 64 below Mr & Mrs Boucquiau's house in Belgium, designed by Mariana Frisenna; 65 left Marianne von Kantzow's shop Solgården in Stockholm; 65 right & 66 above a home featuring Jane Churchill fabrics; 66 below left a house in the Hamptons designed by Solis Betancourt; 66 below right Ann Mollo's house in London; 67 Anthony Cochran's apartment in New York; 68 Walter Gropius House, a property of the Society for the Preservation of New England Antiquities; 69 left Tricia Foley's house on Long Island; 69 right Moussie Sayers of Nordic Style's house in London; 70 Nina Gustafsson's Swedish home; 71 left Peter Hone's apartment in London; 71 right Nina Gustafsson's Swedish home; 72 Mark Gilbey & Polly Dickens' house in Philadelphia; 72-73 Glen Senk & Keith Johnson's house in Philadelphia; 74-75 Anna Bonde of Linum's house in Provence; 77 above left Artists Ben Langlands & Nikki Bell's house in London; 77 above right a house in Suffolk designed by James Gorst; 77 centre left Keith & Cathy Abell's New York house designed by 1100 Architect; 77 centre right Interior by Tuula Poyhonen; 77 below left Mr & Mrs van Hool's kitchen designed by Claire Bataille & Paul Ibens Designs; 77 below right James Gager & Richard Ferretti's New York apartment, designed by Stephen Roberts; 78-79 a home featuring Jane Churchill fabrics; 80-81 Chantal Fabres' apartment in London, photography by Luis Gonzalez Palma and collage by Samy Bemayor, both from Marlborough, Chile and mirror by London Metier; 81 James Gager & Richard Ferretti's New York apartment, designed by Stephen Roberts;

82 above Jerry & Susan Lauren's apartment in New York; 82 below Ralph & Ann Pucci's New York home, furnished in collaboration with Vicente Wolf; 83 Frédéric Méchiche's apartment in Paris; 84 Lena Proudlock's house in Gloucestershire; 85 Interior designer Holly Hunt's home in Chicago; 86 Tristan Auer's apartment in Paris; 87 Susanna Colleoni & Didi Huber's home in Milan; 88 & 89 left Nigel Greenwood's apartment in London; 89 right a home featuring Jane Churchill fabrics; 90 Marina & Ivan Ritossa's Boffi kitchen in London, designed by Alternative Plans; 91 left Weaving/Thomasson residence, London; 91 right Interior by Tuula Poyhonen; 92 Dean Smith & Pearl Wou's home in London; 92-93 Josephine Ryan's house in London; 94-95 an apartment in Brussels designed by Vincent van Duysen; 96 left Robert Kaiser residence, Florida; 96 above right a home featuring Jane Churchill fabrics; 96 below right Glen Senk & Keith Johnson's house in Philadelphia; 97 left Yvonne Sporre's home, designed by J F Desalle; 97 right Jasper Conran's home in London; 98-99 Kristiina Ratia's Connecticut home; 100 left Mr & Mrs van Hool's kitchen designed by Claire Bataille & Paul Ibens Designs; 100 right Maria Reyes Ventos' apartment in Barcelona; 101 Tricia Foley's house on Long Island; 102-103 home of Peri Wolfman & Charles Gold in Bridgehampton; 104 Tricia Foley's house on Long Island; 105 left Anthony Cochran's apartment in New York; 105 right Moussie Sayers of Nordic Style's house in London; 106 House in London by Stickland Coombe Architects; 107 a home featuring Jane Churchill fabrics; 108 left Chantal Fabres' apartment in London; 108 right Ralph & Ann Pucci's New York home, furnished in collaboration with Vicente Wolf; 109 left Frédéric Méchiche's apartment in Paris; 109 right Lena Proudlock's house in Gloucesterhire; 110 Katy Barker's Paris apartment, designed by Laurent Buttazoni; 111 left Lincoln/Orum residence, Suffolk, interior by Angi Lincoln; 111 right Bevan residence, London; 112 above

Martine Colliander of White Sense's apartment in Stockholm; 112 below & 113 Lena Proudlock's house in Gloucestershire; 114 above Stephen Roberts' New York apartment; 114 below Lincoln/Orum residence in Suffolk, interior by Angi Lincoln; 115 above James Mohn & Keith Recker's apartment in New York, architecture by James Mohn and interior design as a collaboration between Keith Recker and James Mohn; 115 below left Vicente Wolf's New York apartment; 115 below right Fishman residence in Florida. Interiors by Wilson Stiles, Sarasota, Florida; 116 Sally Mackereth & Julian Vogel's house in London, designed by Wells Mackereth; 117 Mark Badgley & James Mischka's New York apartment; 118 Kristiina Ratia's Connecticut home; 119 above Lena Proudlock's house in Gloucestershire; 119 below Nina Gustafsson's Swedish home; 120 left Interior Designer Holly Hunt's home in Chicago; 120 right Reed & Delphine Krakoff's Manhattan townhouse, designed by Delphine Krakoff of Pamplemousse Design Inc.; 121 Jasper Conran's home in London; 122 Anna Bonde of Linum's house in Provence; 123 left Marianne von Kantzow of Solgården's house in Stockholm; 123 right Curtains designed by Agnès Comar; 124 a house in New York designed by Shelton, Mindel & Associates; 125 A New York loft designed by architext Jonathan Leitersdorf; 126 Hubert Zandberg's apartment in London; 127 Kristiina Ratia's Connecticut home; 128-129 an apartment in Brussels designed by Vincent van Duysen; 130 above Reed & Delphine Krakoff's Manhattan townhouse, designed by Delphine Krakoff of Pamplemousse Design Inc.; 130 below an apartment in Paris designed by KOLD; 131 Nina Gustafsson's Swedish home; 132 above Katy Barker's Paris apartment designed by Laurent Buttazoni; 132 below an apartment in Paris designed by Frédéric Méchiche; 134 Susanna Colleoni & Didi Huber's home in Milan.

It is always a pleasure to write a book with Jacqui and her
team and this one was no exception; Kate John,
Sian Parkhouse and Ashley Western made the whole
process almost completely painless, and actually, rather fun!